Can't Pay, Won't Pay

Can't Pay, Won't Pay

The Fight to Stop the Poll Tax

Simon Hannah

PLUTO  PRESS

First published 2020 by Pluto Press
345 Archway Road, London N6 5AA

www.plutobooks.com

Copyright © Simon Hannah 2020

The right of Simon Hannah to be identified as the author of this work has been
asserted by him in accordance with the Copyright, Designs and Patents Act 1988.

British Library Cataloguing in Publication Data
A catalogue record for this book is available from the British Library

ISBN   978 0 7453 4085 2   Hardback
ISBN   978 0 7453 4081 4   Paperback
ISBN   978 1 7868 0604 8   PDF eBook
ISBN   978 1 7868 0606 2   Kindle eBook
ISBN   978 1 7868 0605 5   EPUB eBook

Typeset by Stanford DTP Services, Northampton, England

Simultaneously printed in the United Kingdom and United States of America

Dedicated to those who were
imprisoned fighting the Tory Tax

Contents

Preface

As this book was being prepared for publishing, Boris Johnson led the Conservative Party to a decisive electoral victory on 12 December 2019. This defeat sent demoralising shock waves across the left. The spectre of a never-ending Tory government, headed by a narcissistic liar and born-to-rule populist demagogue, left many in despair. This was compounded by the apparent defeat of the politics of the Labour left at the ballot box.

But it is my deepest hope that people draw some inspiration from the political history told in this book. After all, the Tories seemed unassailable by the late 1980s; Thatcher was the victor of three elections in a row and the person who crushed the miners' union. The sense that they couldn't be beaten, that neither Labour nor the powerful British trade unions could make a dent against the Tory juggernaut, was a palpable one.

Despite this, there were people who stuck with the fight, who kept going even through defeat, that proved their mettle at a time when it seemed the forces of history were against them. Those people helped form the backbone to the anti-Poll Tax movement. They established the first anti-Poll Tax Unions, put up the posters, defied the bailiffs and faced potential imprisonment. They were the ones who led much wider forces into battle against the government and eventually won.

It took work, and it ultimately meant not relying on the trade unions or the Labour Party. Don't misunderstand this point, these institutions should not be abandoned as sites of struggle. Often in times of political and social crisis people have to form their own organisations and be prepared to go it alone. Waiting for the Labour Party to actively support a practical struggle has historically been a recipe for paralysis. Indeed, Labour showed in 1992 it could snatch defeat from the jaws of victory quite easily, even after a mass movement dealt the Conservatives a devastating blow.

In the fights to come there is no doubt that there are huge stakes. With a populist, authoritarian, right-wing wave sweeping the globe, standing firm, organising and overcoming a feeling of despair or defeat, is what will make all the difference.

This is the story of the last mass movement in Britain that helped bring down a Tory prime minister. What happens next will be decided by you ... .

Introduction

'In this world nothing can be said to be certain, except death and taxes.'

Benjamin Franklin

In 1990 Trafalgar Square was witness to scenes of violence the like of which had not been seen in central London for a hundred years. It was a cry of sheer frustration and anger at the Conservative Government's 'flagship policy' of the Community Charge – otherwise known as the Poll Tax. The tax was based on a simple principle: that everyone should pay the same for local services, 'a duke as much as a bin man' (or a waste disposal officer in today's parlance). The Poll Tax was the pinnacle of the Thatcherite programme, the epitome of the New Right ideology. But it was subsequently described by Ivor Crewe and Anthony King in their 2013 book, *The Blunders of our Governments*, as 'a colossal blunder. We might be tempted to call it the blunder to end all blunders.'[1] What went wrong?

It was not the riot alone that sank the flagship. It was a mass non-payment campaign, fought on council estates and in communities up and down Britain, which defeated the tax. Alongside the events in Trafalgar Square there were clashes with police outside council chambers, lobbying of councillors, community pickets outside homes to stop bailiffs, hundreds of court appearances, arguments with judges, and prisoner solidarity campaigns. It was the work of thousands of people collectively organising – against the wishes of the Labour Party and the trade union leaders – that achieved success.

The terror of another Poll-Tax-style rebellion remains even 30 years later. Since the Conservatives re-entered government in 2010 there have been several policies that have invited comparison with the ill-fated Community Charge. It is a common refrain for politicians and journalists to warn that some unpopular government measure will be the 'next Poll Tax'. John Major and Gordon Brown both warned that Universal Credit could trigger a similar scale of fight back.[2] Writing for the BBC in 2014, Brian Taylor asked 'Is the "bedroom tax" the new Poll Tax?'[3] Even the RAC claimed 'another poll tax' was brewing when speed camera detection devices were banned in 2000.[4]

None of those government measures, however, provoked a mass popular response. The reason for that was obvious – the Poll Tax affected everyone, whereas changes to welfare benefits, for example, affect only those in receipt of such benefits. Whilst protests and campaigns can emerge from such measures, they lack the generalised nature of the resistance to the Community Charge.

This book is a historical account of the background to the Community Charge and how a mass movement defeated it. It will bring together policy analysis, arguments around the role of the official labour movement, critical appraisals of political tendencies like Militant, the anarchists and the rest of the far left, as well as the day to day work of campaigners, whether on protests or in the courtrooms.

There have been other accounts of the events surrounding the Community Charge, most of them written shortly after the tax was abolished. David Butler, Andrew Adonis and Tony Travers wrote an account of the Poll Tax from the perspective of Whitehall and its failure of governance. Militant activist Tommy Sheridan's account provided a sense of the movement seen through his eyes – an essential account, considering his role in the campaign. Maureen Reynolds, also a Militant member and treasurer of the All Britain Anti-Poll Tax Federation, produced a very useful report of her experiences, focused on the North West. From an anarchist perspective, Bristol-based Danny Burns's pamphlet *Poll Tax Rebellion* adds a helpful counter-balance to some of the mainstream left's narratives. The story presented in this book will bring all these threads together, from the machinations of Whitehall to the resistance on estates in places like Pollok.

The book starts from the view that the mass movement against the Poll Tax was a decisive factor in ending the policy. It examines the role of the campaign in the political backlash that led to Thatcher's resignation in November 1990. It also tackles some of the more difficult questions, such as why a mass movement that helped bring down Thatcher and abolish a hated tax still saw the Conservatives win the General Election in 1992. Alongside the authors of all the books, articles and pamphlets cited in the text I want to thank all the people who gave interviews, provided materials and photos as well as everyone who read draft chapters and gave feedback. Any errors are of course mine.

To provide some historical context for why the question of taxation is not a dry and boring subject but has, on occasion, sparked riots, revolts and revolutions, we will begin with a brief history of taxes and why people have refused them.

1

A Brief History of Tax Resistance and Revolutions

Everyone complains about taxes: that they are too high, that other people should be paying more, or that tax revenue is not being properly spent by the government. Some people even complain that taxes exist at all – they think all government is tyranny and that we should be left to the tender mercies of the free market and our individual capacities. The concept of a government taking money from the people it rules over is, however, as old as government itself; indeed, it is what provides the financial basis for the political and administrative rulers of our lives. Many of the earliest tax revenues were not allocated on the basis of need, but were used to pay for military adventures or grand palaces for despots. Securing taxes from the lower orders often involved barbaric violence from armed men – the dreaded bailiffs – would arrive at your door and demand payment on behalf of the local lord or the king. For many people their only experience of government was this seizing of their money or goods as taxes.

This process was often bound up with religion too. The tithes you would pay to the church were bound up with a financial obligation to save your mortal soul – better to pay what little you had now than languish in hell for all eternity. In the Islamic states a special tax known as the *Jizyah* was levied on non-believers. In the Holy Roman Empire, Jews, who were considered the property of the Crown, had to pay an additional tax known as the *Leibzoll*. This was paid so that Jews would be 'tolerated' in European countries. It was still being levied in some places in the early nineteenth century. Others enjoyed a privileged position when it came to tax – the scribes of Ancient Egypt, for example, avoided conscription or hard labour in return for administering taxation on behalf of the pharaohs.

Because taxation is so bound up with the social and political order – it being the primary way in which people engaged with their rulers before the introduction of liberal democracy – it often throws into sharp relief some of the contradictions at the heart of societies. Taxes are essentially a political question. As such, the question of taxation has on occasion caused massive social upheaval. The most famous example is that of Britain's American colonies. The British government wanted to assert its right to tax the colonies, extracting finance from them just as they extracted raw materials from colonial lands. When the government allowed the British East India Company to trade tea from England without customs tax, while imposing onerous taxes on American colonists (backed up by soldiers and warships), the pro-independence Sons of Liberty threw crates of tea into the sea at the Boston docks. In the 1770s, the slogan 'no taxation without representation!' expressed the colonists' anger at being subjects of a king and parliament over the sea while having no say in the laws governing their own communities. Thus began a revolutionary struggle for independence that culminated in the formation of what became the most powerful capitalist country in the world.

The British too have a long history of grievances against overbearing taxation. There is the famous legend of Lady Godiva, a noblewoman in the eleventh century who was so distressed by her husband's excessive taxation on the people that she begged him to reduce them. He agreed to do so only if she rode naked through the streets to prove her commitment to the cause. Sitting naked on a horse, her body shrouded only by her long hair, her act of public shame persuaded her husband to lower the taxes.

The English Civil War began in large part over a dispute between the Crown and Parliament over who could levy taxes and for what ends. It was a revolutionary struggle waged by the nascent British bourgeoisie, struggling against the stifling restrictions of the feudalist monarchy and seeking a degree of sovereignty over their own affairs. The resulting conflict changed the course of history and led to the only period in British history in which there was no monarch on the throne. As also illustrated by previous conflicts like the German Peasant War, the right to raise taxes is inseparable from the question of who has control – of who the ruling class is and what kind of state they can create.

Rebellions over tax collection were recorded in Worcester in 1041, in Scotland in 1725 (over taxes on malt) and across England in 1733, when Prime Minister Robert Walpole imposed an excise tax on goods which infuriated shopkeepers and traders. That particular crisis was again caused by Parliament needing to raise money for its wars as the national debt was ballooning, meaning that more revenue streams had to be found. Since import and export tariffs on goods were usually raised at docks, this had the effect of encouraging smuggling on an almost industrial scale. In response, Walpole proposed excise duties that gave extensive powers of search and seizure to tax officials as they checked goods not at the port of entry but in warehouses or even shops. Petitions to MPs gave way to angry protests and the threat of a possible uprising, causing Walpole to withdraw the excise duties. Claiming that 'the act could not be carried into execution without an armed force, and that there would be an end of the liberties of England if supplies were to be raised by the sword',[1] Walpole only obscured the fact that throughout history tax collection has always ultimately been a question of force and power, just as government is more generally.

Another tax whose results can still be seen today was the Window Tax of 1696, an 'assessed tax' which was a way of squeezing the upper classes. The seventeenth-century gentry who flaunted their wealth with powdered wigs, male servants (far more expensive to keep than female servants) and large houses with many windows, found themselves taxed on all these items. Some thrifty well-to-do bricked up their windows to frustrate government officials. These bricked windows are a sight you can still see today in some parts of Britain.

Such examples aside, the burden of taxation has often fallen on those least able to pay. The early nineteenth century was dominated by issues around taxation, another symptom of the growing strength of the capitalist class and their struggles with the aristocratic landowners and their own working classes. The hugely expensive Napoleonic Wars had bled most people dry. The many resulting economic and social issues were compounded by the disastrous 1816 'year without a summer' (also known as 'eighteen hundred and starve to death'), when crops failed after the sun was blotted out by a volcanic eruption the year before in Indonesia. In addition, the Corn Laws – a mixture of tariffs and outright bans on imported grain – led to artificially high food prices, all to preserve the profits of the big landowners. In those days the majority of wages was spent on bread because it made up the bulk of working people's diets. The clamour for constitutional and political reform grew louder. The government responded with violent suppression: the riots at Spa Fields in 1816, and the Peterloo massacre of 1819.

The crop failures and high food prices led to an upsurge in the Radical Press – newspapers with an explicitly liberal message, usually paid for by industrialists struggling against government policy that they felt favoured the landowners over the capitalist class. The government retaliated with a newspaper tax in 1815, intended to price such publications out of the hands of the urban poor. This led to the creation of 'penny papers': cheap mass-produced newspapers designed for popular consumption, the *Poor Man's Guardian* being the most famous. Pioneering radical journalists like William Cobbett wrote disparagingly about the 'tax-eaters', the bloated and corrupt sinecures, who lavished money to 'build new palaces and pull down others, and to pay loan-mongers and all that enormous tribe; and to be expended in various other ways not at all necessary to the well-being of the nation'.[2]

People fought back. The Anti-Corn Laws League (ACLL) was led by John Bright and Richard Cobden, one a liberal manufacturer, the other a Quaker and noted orator – some said the best of his day. Their campaign recruited mass forces, vying with the far more radical Chartist movement for support among working people. The Corn Laws were eventually repealed in 1846, representing a victory for the industrial classes and their free trade cause. The repeal brought cheaper food but also ushered in an economic boom which strengthened the forces of industrialisation and commercialisation in Britain.

For the purposes of this book, however, the most famous historical precedent for a Poll Tax (essentially a tax on people) in Britain occurred in 1377–81. The young Richard II imposed the new tax on everyone to help fund the Hundred Years War against France – at that point in its 43rd year. The Poll Tax was levied repeatedly, with the amount growing each year and the peasants' ability to pay getting harder. More people were vanishing into the woods to become outlaws in order to escape the tax officials. A mass uprising saw peasant armies from Kent and Essex invade London, behead the king's Chancellor and the Archbishop of Canterbury, and burn down the homes of the rich. The uprising was brutally put down and its leaders hung, drawn and quartered – the fate of all traitors to the Crown. However the fear that the uprising provoked in the ruling elites meant that the idea of a Poll Tax imposed on the masses was finished for over 600 years.

That is, until the Conservative government of Margaret Thatcher. It is a surprise, then, that by the time Thatcher came to consider the Community Charge in the 1980s, she had not learnt from history that it can be perilous to play around with taxes.

The moral economy

Taxation is, in its simplest form, a political question of the redistribution of resources and wealth. Taxes presuppose some kind of money economy (or at least commodities that can be seized in kind) and the existence of a state with a bureaucracy that requires funds in order to operate. As a general rule, the more complex the state the more complex the tax arrangements. And as history demonstrates, the political question of taxation is one which derives both from the practical realities of the governing apparatus requiring funds and the philosophical basis of that apparatus. As human society developed and the concept of individual rights and social contracts became more commonplace, the idea of governing by consent and not by explicit force meant that taxation had to be carefully considered and calculated by the ruling classes. As a result taxes can be either *regressive*, based on onerous calculations over who should pay which target the poorest, or *progressive*, based on sliding scales linked to ability to pay or specifically targeted at the rich through wealth, capital or corporation taxes. Taxes at their worst involve the powerful bleeding dry the lower classes for their own designs, while at their best they lead to a degree of social cohesion based on the state paying for welfare and healthcare, an approach that became synonymous with European social democracy.

There are times, however, when the priorities and needs of people become dislocated from the legal framework of the ruling class. When that happens people decide their own rules on a community level. There is a popular term for this that both historians and sociologists like to use: the moral economy. This refers to the way that ethical questions govern everyday economic decisions ranging from consumerism to economic production itself. It might be part of the moral economy to steal, if you are starving. An early win, indeed arguably the key win for the Anti-Poll Tax movement, was to clearly embed opposition to the tax in the context of a moral economy, such that it became a *good and a right* not to pay it.

Edward P. Thompson writes about the role of the moral economy in *The Making of the English Working Class*, focusing chiefly on the importance of the apparently spontaneous outbreak of mass resistance and direct action. Thompson uses the example of bread riots in reaction to shopkeepers putting up prices during shortages to make more profit.

The intense anger about this tapped into 'traditional' forms of moral economy: that it is wrong to profiteer from poverty, that there are bonds of community more important than making some extra cash from desperate people. In Thompson's words: 'behind every such form of popular direct action some legitimising notion of right is to be found.'[3] Taking that as a starting point we can see that the Anti-Poll Tax movement also fostered a strong moral economy, harkening back to older traditions of popular resistance, and even invoking the near revolution of 1381. The notion of a *right* to refuse to pay an onerous tax became a material force in the minds of millions.

In such ways the question of fairness comes to dominate the national debate. People will generally put up with all manner of deprivations and suffering if they believe that it is somehow right to do so. Naturally what is considered fair over time changes as society moves to the left or the right on any given political question. In one context people may think it is fair to take in refugees and those suffering from oppression and wars abroad. In another context those same people might consider an influx of foreigners to be an outrage and a scandal. The same applies to the evolving social contract with the government.

Taxes are inevitably seen through this prism of fairness, in terms of the moral economy of whether it is right or just to pay a tax and who pays it. This is not to conceive of taxes in a simple liberal sense: in a bourgeois democracy the concept of fairness is a complex one, run through with class politics. Fairness in a class-based society is a complicated issue. Clearly, an economy that allows some people to get rich beyond any reasonable measure of need, while others are made homeless or rely on food banks, is not a 'fair' society. Nevertheless, ideologically, the notion that our capitalist society is rooted in human nature, and that our rulers have a right to rule while we have a right to vote for who rules us, is a hegemonic belief.

The taxation our rulers impose on us is a class question, but it is always mediated by the general sense of a just and right balance of responsibility. In the 1970s, income tax on the very rich was 83 per cent, a price that – it was argued – had to be paid for wealth redistribution and funding the welfare state. It was Thatcher's great revolution (alongside Ronald Reagan in the United States) to rapidly reduce the top rate of income tax – today it stands at levels of around 20 per cent. The rich now believe that it is 'unfair' to ask them to pay more. This is why

tax dodging by corporations and tax evasion by the super-rich are politically charged issues – if they become too widespread they create a sense
of unfairness and therefore begin to erode the legitimacy of the ruling
class. The hegemony can falter and crack. As such, the first question to
ask when it comes to a historical account of the Poll Tax is: why was the
tax not considered fair?

2

Why a Poll Tax?

'There is an alternative. A poll tax is clearly feasible, fair and desirable. What is needed now is the political will to introduce it.'

Michael Forsyth, Conservative MP

The 1980s in Britain was a decade of the haves and the have-nots. Thatcher sold people a fantasy of self-reliance and individualism that was the closest Britain ever got to its own version of the American Dream. Some people got very rich and saw substantial improvements in their standard of living. This was the 'loadsamoney' generation: yuppies, stockbrokers and speculators enjoying life after the Big Bang of financial deregulation, flaunting their wealth with pin-striped suits and mobile phones that had batteries the size of large bricks. Some sections of the working class who bought their own homes or who sought to escape their class background cashed in on the new money economy, flash boys looking to make a buck from the rolling back of the public sector. To grease the palms of the rich further, the top rate of income tax was steadily cut throughout the decade in successive budgets.

Britain did not have a Wild West mythology to fall back on, so the new frontier to tame was the inner cities, populated by the urban poor. They became the equivalent of the bandits and 'savages' of White American folklore. By the mid-1980s the Tories were riding high on a short-lived economic boom fuelled by cheap credit and tax cuts. Privatisation had boosted some businesses, and the deregulation of the City of London was being heralded across the media as a bold and revolutionary step towards making Britain a finance capital powerhouse. The miners had been beaten and the left in local government had been crushed. The New Right had convinced a generation of their vision. All that was needed was their continued votes and their faith that the rewards would eventually come.

But for the poorest 10 per cent life did not improve. They earned on average £151.58 a week in 1979 but only £158.57 in 1990 – an increase of just 4.6 per cent. Child poverty doubled during Thatcher's reign, from 1.7 million in 1979 to 3.3 million in 1990 – an increase from 13 per cent to 30 per cent.[1] Some parts of the country were economically abandoned, notably in the North. Industrial centres where generations of families had worked the docks, forged steel or dug coal were reduced to bitter deprivation and generational cycles of poverty and drug abuse. People did not just lose jobs when the economy went into recession – entire industries were gone for good. Structural unemployment blighted many parts of Britain, peaking at nearly 12 per cent in 1984, the year the miners' strike started, before falling to 6.9 per cent in 1990. Considering that the Tories had fought the 1979 election on the slogan 'Labour isn't working', this might be seen as a bitter historical irony.

The Tory attacks on trade unions and destruction of long-established industries meant that a number of workers ended up in worse-paid jobs or were unemployed. By 1989, 6 million people in work were also in poverty. The Breadline Britain survey found that 'in 1983 14% of households lacked three or more necessities because they could not afford them. That proportion had increased to 21% in 1990.'[2] Child poverty, a measure of the income levels of families more generally, had risen from 13 per cent in 1979 to 22 per cent in 1990. By nearly every measure poverty and deprivation had grown during Conservative rule in the 1980s. In cities like Manchester, stagnant benefit rates, increases in bills for electricity, gas and water, and ten years of cuts to local government services had all had a serious impact on the quality of life for thousands of people.[3]

But Thatcher had also disproved one apparently iron law of elections: that you can't win if unemployment is going up. Unemployment was sky-rocketing in 1983, but Thatcher veritably slaughtered Labour at the general election. Of course, the 1983 election was overdetermined by the recent victory against Argentina in the Falklands War, as well as the formation of the SDP which split the Labour vote and handed seats to the Tories. But the election also saw more working-class voters put a cross in the box for a political party other than Labour for the first time since 1945. Thatcher won again in 1987, with 3.2 million still unemployed, many long term. She had captured the mood of a nation worn down by the crisis of social democracy, the global economic shocks of the 1970s and the growing sense of national decline. But Thatcher proposed more poison to cure the ailment, pushing the industrial and economic decline to its limit while promising that a brave new world would be built on the broken back of the old one. Enough people were willing to buy this snake-oil remedy to ensure her continued domination of UK politics.

Of course this has to be contextualised. Thatcher won landslides in Parliament but her vote still represented only 31 per cent of the electorate. There were several times when her rule was challenged, both from within the Tories but also through mass opposition on the streets and on picket lines. Nevertheless she fought on determinedly. Under the first-past-the-post system, her grip on the legislature allowed her to implement fundamental political, social and economic changes. This was the triumph of the New Right, with its new realism that the market was supreme and the state was inevitably a monstrous waste, a bureaucratic monster blocking the way of economic progress. This ideology was always advocated with a degree of hypocrisy, however. Thatcher waged war on local government and the unions to prevent their interference in the market, but also strengthened the state at the same time: Westminster could impose local spending limits, and the police could beat strikers at will.

Much has been written about Thatcher's war on the unions, but she also sought to control and curtail local government. Her experiences as Minister for Education under Ted Heath in the 1970–74 government had convinced her that many councils were too big, unwieldy, inefficient and implicitly socialistic. She had watched powerlessly as local councils undertook a bold policy of turning grammar schools into comprehensives – something she instinctively opposed but was unable to halt.[4] The opposition from teachers and local councils when she scrapped milk for school children – leading to her infamous 'milk snatcher' label – had stung her deeply.

As Prime Minister, Thatcher had the power to wage a personal and vindictive war against local government, inspired by New Right theory that identified it as a breeding ground for socialism. Britain had enjoyed a long-term if somewhat inconsistent constitutional arrangement between 1600 and 1979, wherein local government had a degree of autonomy from Westminster, but Thatcher took her election victories as a sign that it was time for the cosy arrangement to come to an end. This initially alienated many of her peers who stood in the tradition of Tory municipality, on the side of local, decentralised and autonomous politics. They were dubbed the 'wets', enemies within that had to be overcome.

This is the first point to understand – the Poll Tax was designed to be the triumphant final nail in the coffin of local government as any kind of progressive instrument of wealth redistribution. It was also intended to finally end the spectre of radical left-wing councils, thereby inoculating the electorate against socialism. By capping their spending and forcing them to privatise their services, the new arrangement was designed to rid local government of any remaining socialist tendencies forever, turning working-class voters against their Labour councillors in the process.

The people behind the Poll Tax

The basic idea for the Community Charge had been slowly growing for several years. Historically, local government was funded through various streams: the local rates (essentially a tax on the nominal rental value of a property), local business rates, the Revenue Support Grant (money from central government), and any additional local revenue from, for instance, parking charges, rent incomes or regional grants. The rating system had been around in some form for hundreds of years, though both Labour and the Conservatives had made noises about either reforming it or scrapping it entirely. The system was inequitable, unpopular and arguably anachronistic – on that much there was a measure of agreement.

The rates had gone through periodic revaluations to make sure they did not fall too far behind socio-economic changes – the last one had been in 1974. This usually led to grumbles from Middle England, whose houses were worth the most and therefore they had to shoulder most of the tax burden. Such was the Tories' fear of the impact on their voters if they undertook their own rate revaluation in the early 1980s that when Michael Heseltine raised the issue with Thatcher she replied bluntly: 'we are not doing it'. Since rating revaluation notices had already been dispatched, Heseltine got to put on a public show urging people to just rip up their forms and put them in the bin. No one knew at the time that this would be a prelude to hundreds of thousands of people ripping up their Poll Tax forms years later.

The Conservative Party had pledged to abolish the rates system as far back as October 1974. Ironically, considering what came next, one of their main arguments had been that the system was coming 'under increasing criticism because it does not reflect people's ability to pay'.[5] During the 1970s the party shifted its position and argued that the rate system was unfair. An elderly (potentially Tory-voting) pensioner might live in a house with neighbours who were working and earning considerably more money, yet had to pay more even though she had less money to do so. The Tories – publicly anyway – initially argued that the rates were regressive as they were not based on ability to pay. Someone might have a big house but very little income – so how could the system be fair?

The issue was what to replace the rates with. The rating system had existed in one form or another since 1601. It was clunky and occasionally unfair, but people knew what it was and local councils had control over what level to set it at (until rate capping in 1985). The other potential options all had their benefits and drawbacks, as is common with any financial levy system. The alternatives proposed included a local income tax, a sales tax and a property tax. In the 1970s, a draft Parliamentary Green Paper had included the idea of a per capita tax – a tax on heads – but only to rubbish it as an unworkable proposal.

It was not until 1981 that an official Green Paper, *Alternatives to Domestic Rates*, came out that put a per capita tax forward as a proposal on an equal footing with the others. Even then, the civil servants who helped draft it did not think it was viable; they decided to include it merely for 'completion's sake'. One prescient Treasury official remarked of the Poll Tax: 'try collecting that in Brixton!'[6] Brixton had just seen serious riots in April of that year, and the picture of it as an untamed Dodge City haunted the establishment imagination. When news of the proposal got out, the Labour frontbench were adamant in their opposition. Gerald Kaufman, Labour's Spokesperson on the Environment, was quoted as saying Labour would 'fight tooth and nail' any moves by the government to introduce such a tax.[7]

It also isn't a coincidence that the British government had been implementing a poll tax for several decades before the 1950s, just not in Britain. The tax had been the favoured method of funding colonial administrations in African colonies, alongside a 'Hut Tax', since the late nineteenth century. First introduced in Ghana, it was then imposed on colonised peoples in Kenya, Uganda, Nyasaland, Eastern Nigeria, Northern Rhodesia, Tanganyika and Sierra Leone.[8] The colonial mindset of the rich politician sitting in Whitehall can be applied equally to Sub-Saharan Africa as it can to inner-city London. Academics who studied the impact of the poll tax in the colonies concluded that it was 'inequitable and regressive, and ... perceived as unfair by citizens. There is often widespread unwillingness to pay. Non-compliance is a serious problem.'[9]

In November 1984 the idea of a poll tax remained unpopular among civil servants. The push came from Patrick Jenkin, the Secretary of State for the Environment (which covered local government), after he had been criticised for not being tough enough with the Greater London Council and Ken Livingstone. As a result of his perceived weaknesses he was replaced in 1985 by Kenneth Baker. Thatcher's obsession with replacing the rates led her to set up an ad hoc task force, rather than an official intergovernmental committee, because she feared that the civil service, and in particular her Chancellor Nigel Lawson, would try and block anything too radical. This was an unprecedented break from the usual procedures in such matters. Parliamentary under-secretary William Waldegrave set up a high-powered team of hand-picked experts to report directly to him, though Kenneth Baker managed to inveigle himself into some of the discussions.

This semi-clandestine group was called the Local Government Finance (LGF) team. It included High Court Judge Sir Leonard Hoffman, Lord Victor Rothschild, Oliver Letwin MP and Christopher Foster, an LSE lecturer in economics. Thatcher took no direct part in the deliberations, but made it clear that they had to come up with an alternative to the rates – the status quo was not an option. The team was sworn to secrecy, and forbidden from reporting their work to any government department, especially the Treasury.[10]

Sometime between December 1984 and March 1985, Thatcher herself had become convinced of both the value and the feasibility of introducing a poll tax. After Waldegrave's team had done their work and modelled a proposal called the 'Residence Tax', she convened a high-level meeting at Chequers in the spring of 1985 to present the idea in a serious manner. The meeting was held just as the miner's strike was winding down to defeat and the local government left was about to be crushed in its attempt to resist rate capping. The sense of triumphalism from the Tories was palpable. Half the Cabinet attended, but crucially Nigel Lawson was away at the time, leaving a powerful opposition voice out of the discussion. Mysteriously, no one had been briefed prior to the meeting, and barely anyone in the Cabinet knew what was to be on the agenda that day. It was at this fateful meeting in March 1985 that Waldegrave and Baker presented their idea to the inner circle of the Thatcherite government to establish a 'fair' tax that would treat everyone the same. The presentation, full of management speak was replete with flip charts, dubious graphs and coloured slide projections that proved the various things they were intended to prove. The learned men concluded that a poll tax was not only legitimate, it was actually preferable as a means of funding local government. Waldegrave then appealed to the Prime Minister's vanity by concluding that if she adopted the Community Charge then 'you will have fulfilled your promise to abolish the rates'[11] – a promise first made at the 1974 election. After a pregnant pause, Thatcher turned to her assembled ministers and asked; 'I am convinced by the arguments of William and Kenneth. What do you think?'[12]

Of course, what the 1974 Conservative manifesto had promised was not a flat-rate capitation tax; if anything it was the opposite: 'within the normal lifetime of a Parliament we shall abolish the domestic rating system and replace it by taxes *more broadly based and related to people's ability to pay*. Local authorities must continue to have some independent source of finance.'[13]

It was around this time that the right-wing Adam Smith Institute (ASI) published a pamphlet calling for a capitation tax (a tax on people) to fund local services. Douglas Mason, a lecturer in economics at St Andrews University, the Tory leader of Kirkcaldy Council and a libertarian, authored a pamphlet for the ASI called *Revising the Ratings System*, which offers a very interesting insight into Thatcherite ideology. For the Conservatives in the 1980s, fairness meant treating people equally in a society where there is no equality. This is what led to the infamous remark on the Community Charge made by arch-Thatcherite Nicholas Ridley: 'why would a duke pay more than a dustman? It is only because we have been subjected to socialist ideas for the last 50 years that people think this is fair.'[14] Thatcher saw it as an opportunity to change the heart and soul of a people. She wrote in her memoirs that the goal was to 'turn dependents into citizens', to make people care more about local council politics by connecting it far more directly with their wallets and purses.[15] The principle was that everyone would pay something, even if it was heavily rebated.

It is worth noting that these views ran contrary to the principles of taxation as advocated by the early economic theorist of capitalism, Adam Smith, who had argued that 'the subjects of every state ought to contribute towards the support of the government as nearly as possible in proportion to their respective abilities.'[16] But what Smith had believed was ignored by those who invoked his name. The ASI pamphlet was not decisive in shifting the conversation, but it was part of the growing clamour for a poll tax from the intellectual networks that had been established by the outlier neoliberal right since the early 1970s.

Right-wing Thatcherites were very excited about the prospect of such a revolution in local government finance. The Secretary of State for

Scotland, George Younger, was initially a keen proponent; on hearing that a poll tax was being seriously considered he allegedly exclaimed 'all my political life I have been waiting for this!'[17] What became the Community Charge was first put to the Cabinet on 6 January 1986. This was a different version to the one that was eventually implemented. It was to be gradually phased in over a decade, in a process called 'dual-running', and a safety net would be introduced to redistribute some public money lower spending areas to higher spending ones.

The proposal was agreed within 15 minutes.

The speed with which it was adopted was in part due to a historic coincidence – this was the same Cabinet meeting at which Michael Heseltine stormed out over the Westland Affair. Heseltine's departure left everyone distracted but also removed one of the 'big beasts' who would later become most publicly associated with opposition to the tax. Heseltine's role in the political battle that followed is a somewhat unique one. He was a leading Tory during a period in which how Thatcher viewed you was decisive: you were either 'one of us' or a 'wet'. Heseltine defied such categories. He had pioneered the early war against local government and got his hands dirty battering the Labour left in the council chambers, but he was also an old-school corporatist, and his political hero was the Liberal Prime Minister Lloyd George.[18] He was considered a relic of the more moderate Heath era, at a time when monetarism and a vicious class-war politics dictated the agenda of the Tory Party. Of course, the workers' movement had viewed Heath – with his notorious Industrial Relations Act – as a vicious class enemy. The TUC almost called a general strike against him, so such a legacy should be seen in the historical context. Nevertheless, in the relentless Tory march towards the New Right vision of local government, Heseltine proved to be first an unreliable ally, then a powerful backbench oppositionist as the battle lines were drawn. In his speech against the bill in Parliament he argued that the Community Charge was flawed because 'in the eyes of the tax collector [it equated] the rich and the poor, the slum dweller and the landed aristocrat, the elderly pensioners living on their limited savings and the most successful of today's entrepreneurs'.[19]

There were other opponents within the Cabinet, notably Nigel Lawson and Foreign Secretary Geoffrey Howe, and the popular Leader of the House, John Biffen. It was during one particularly aggressive exchange, when Thatcher rounded on Howe after he criticised the Community Charge, that Biffen did the unthinkable and interrupted her mid-flow. This led to a barrage of invective from Thatcher which Biffen uncharacteristically responded to in kind. He left the Cabinet meeting shaking with anger and was reshuffled out of his role a year later. He later declared of the Poll Tax: 'She called it her flagship. I called it the *Titanic*.'[20] The divisions were clear, but Thatcher was in no mood to entertain opposition.

One of the architects of the tax, Christopher Foster, noted later that he had been horrified at the lack of discussion at Chequers on the conditions attached to the possibility of the tax, in particular its collectability and its potential regressiveness. Because the briefing was held in such paranoid secrecy, Thatcher had pushed through the proposals without sufficient time being set aside to discuss the implications of the changes.[21]

Other Tories opposed the tax for different reasons. The right-wing firebrand Alan Clarke MP was concerned about the proposals for practical reasons, noting in his diary that a strategy of turning dependents into tax payers into citizens was flawed: 'No one will pay. By no one I mean all the slobs, yobs, drifters, junkies, freeloaders, claimants and criminals on day release who make their living by exploitation of the benefits system and overload local authority expenditure. As usual the burden will fall on the thrifty, the prudent, the responsible, those of "fixed address", who patiently support society and the follies of the chattering class.'[22]

How it would work

The new financial arrangements were to be known as the Community Charge. The name was important – it was explicitly not supposed to be a *tax*, but a charge for using local services. You were charged more the more local services there were. This aimed to fix what the Conservatives saw as an iniquity – that you paid tax on the value of your home not the level of services you used. Someone living in a big house who had a job and only used the local bin collections and occasionally the parks was paying far more than an unemployed person on welfare who might have complex needs, be accessing social services, attending community centres and relying on meals-on-wheels and so on. In essence the Conservatives disapproved of the fact that some local tax payers were subsidising others. The new Community Charge was to be geared around the notion of who benefits, not the ability to pay, and it was here that its regressive nature became apparent to the poorer sections of society, since postwar social democracy had been in large part predicated on the notion that the rich should pay more for universal services.

In every local authority the elected representatives would set a personal Community Charge for local residents over the age of 18, which would make up 25 per cent of local funding. There were some exceptions, for instance the mentally ill or the homeless. People who were on benefits were also expected to pay but could get a rebate of up to 80 per cent.

The law stipulated that people living as couples were jointly liable for each other's tax, and that if you were on a low income but lived with a partner on a higher income then you could not get a rebate. Many couples would be hit especially hard by the tax. Due to joint and several liability, if your combined income was more than £165 a week then you both had to the pay the full charge even if one of you was unemployed. The criteria for deciding what counted as a couple were outlined by Michael Portillo as follows:

1. Whether they are in the same household
2. Whether the relationship is a stable one
3. Whether there is mutual financial support
4. Whether there is a sexual relationship
5. Whether they have children in common
6. Whether they are publicly acknowledged as a couple[23]

Additionally, students also had to pay the full amount when they were home for the summer, but only 20 per cent when studying during term time.

The Community Charge was an inherently neoliberal policy because it was rooted in the belief that democratic accountability is best driven by consumer choice. It was intended to introduce a consumer choice mechanism into voting: the cost of council-provided services would send a market signal to local voters about who to vote for. The electorate would supposedly calculate that Labour meant higher tax and more spending on services that lots of local people might not be using (such as a lesbian and gay community centre), whereas the Conservatives were more frugal and only spent money on general services for everyone, like bin collection. Vote Labour if you want it to cost a lot. Vote Tory if you want to keep the pound in your pocket. Naturally this was dressed up in the more acceptable language of civic virtue, citizenship and duty.

The insistence on it being a charge and not a tax also played into this ideology. One unnamed Conservative backbencher justified it to a journalist, claiming that since 'the Duke of Westminster [pays] the same price as a bus driver for a packet of cornflakes, there is no reason why he should not pay the same amount for local authority services'.[24] Likening taxes to the purchasing of cereal is an ideological ploy designed to obscure the political and social nature of taxation, reducing everything to a commodity purchase – paying for a social worker becomes the same as buying some milk.

The Poll Tax was imbued with the language of Thatcherism, that of consumer choice, value for money and the power to choose. These stock phrases were all part of an anti-statist rhetoric intended to undermine Labourism and re-empower voters as consumers united under the banner of the free market. Indeed, it is a measure of how powerful the impact of Thatcherism was that such concepts still dominate British political discourse.[25]

Of course all legislation needs enforcement, so the Conservatives proposed that councils would be empowered to send in sheriffs (in Scotland) or bailiffs (in England and Wales) to collect debts that were owed to them. In England and Wales it was also possible to imprison people for up to three months if they refused to pay their Community Charge.

Alongside the Community Charge the government proposed a Unified Business Rate (UBR) to take taxation of local businesses entirely out of the hands of local government and place it under the control of Westminster. This was an essential plank of the strategy to undermine supposed 'chancellors mini-socialist' in town halls up and down the country who might levy higher taxation on local capitalists to spend on residents services or their workforce. The UBR was set at 36p in the £1 value of the premises for each business, clearly something that would favour the bigger shops and multinational chains and result in higher charges for the independent local shopkeepers.[26]

As with many aspects of the Thatcherite agenda, there was a large degree of counter-veiling hypocrisy to achieve the necessary end. Under the guise of rolling back the state, the UBR policy represented a massive expansion of central state control and oversight. Simon Jenkins later described it as 'the biggest single act of true nationalisation ever undertaken by a British government'.[27] Lord Andrew Mackintosh branded it 'simply another example of central government extending their powers further and further into every reach of our national life at the expense of local government and at the expense of local democracy.'[28] And claims that the reforms were intended to boost local government autonomy were fatally undermined by the continued capping of overspending councils, an imposition by central government that ran against the entire spirit of the reforms.

Arguments against the Community Charge

There were a number of arguments against the tax, which only hardened as the attempt to make people pay it wore on. Whether the tax was a success or not rested largely on the battle of narratives, in particular on who could best convincingly describe the rationale behind the tax. For the left there was a very simple line of argument, as described by Michael Lavalette and Gerry Mooney: 'The Poll Tax was a clear piece of class legislation. By treating all adults over the age of 18 as equals it attempted to reinforce the vast social and economic inequalities of wealth and power in society. The effect was to increase further the burden of paying for local welfare services on to the working class and to undermine any notion that tax should be related to income, wealth and ability to pay.'[29] Labour MP and Militant supporter Dave Nellist described it simply as 'Robin Hood in reverse – a wealth transfusion from the poor to the rich.'[30] Tory MP William Waldegrave admitted later that 'it was impossible to argue against the widespread impression of a huge shift to the better off, because it was true.'[31] Other opponents pointed to a central, humanist ethical consideration: you could tax property, profit, purchases and possessions, but you could not tax people.

Then there was the mechanics of the proposed tax itself. The joint and several liability of couples was also challenged by campaigners: What if a woman was living with a man after divorcing? What if there was domestic violence or controlling behaviour? How would the council determine who counted as co-habiting 'couples'? Would estates be filled with sex snoopers to see if people were copulating on a regular basis? Jo Richardson MP made a strong feminist case against the tax: 'women, who are almost half the labour force, still earn less than three quarters of men's average pay. The government's refusal to take account of ability to pay the flat rate poll tax is blatant discrimination against women.'[32]

There was also serious concern for the plight of carers, the majority of whom were women. At the time there were 6 million people caring for those with disabilities or the elderly in their own homes. Around 1.6 million of these carers were essentially needed 24 hours a day, severely limiting their ability to earn money. Having a disabled family member or a pensioner at home could mean households having to pay more than under the previous rates system, even with the 20 per cent rebate applied.

There were also racial aspects to the Community Charge. Black and Minority Ethnic families were on average larger than their white counterparts. Larger households were far more likely to lose out compared to the rates. The Chartered Institute of Public Finance and Accountancy (CIPFA) warned that 'the Asian community may consider that the Government's proposals, added to other pressures on their traditional way of life, could lead to the breakdown of the family unit'.[33] Black families were often larger but paid lower wages and young Black men were far more likely to be unemployed, creating a scissor crisis in each household of a high Poll Tax and low income. Additionally, the tracking down of people to put them on a register could also prove 'highly sensitive for those living in political exile or with refugee status'.[34] There was also the metropolitan issue, namely that more BAME people lived in big cities, and big cities would have a higher Community Charge – on a population which was historically worse paid than their white neighbours. The Association of London Authorities (ALA) estimated that 92 per cent of ethnic minority households would lose out in Inner London.[35]

Delegitimising the tax was crucial. Popularising the nickname 'Poll Tax' as opposed to Community Charge was an early win, with even journalists regularly calling it by its nickname. The government's propaganda machine fought to make people think of it as a 'charge' and not a tax failed, as most people understood that generally you pay taxes to a council or a government. The Poll Tax label was so established even in 1987 that Thatcher herself famously referred to her flagship policy as such in the Commons.[36] In a government leaflet from 1989 they effectively conceded defeat in the war over the name when they grudgingly referred to it as 'the so-called Poll Tax'.[37]

The next battle was over who would be blamed for a tax that could be very high. Thatcher hoped that people would blame their 'profligate' Labour local councils for the high cost of the tax in urban areas, while the movement had to convince enough people that any high costs were the fault of the Tories. This would sow deeper divisions within the Tory ranks, with Heseltine himself voicing the concerns of some backbenchers during a debate on the tax in Parliament: 'Responsibility for the Poll

Tax will be targeted precisely and unavoidably at the Government who introduced the tax. That tax will be known as "the Tory tax".[38] Could the movement ensure that across Britain people hated the government for the tax rather than the local councils implementing it?

Alongside its general unfairness, the method of collection also came under scrutiny. It involved the creation of a database in each local authority to track every resident. The information would first be collected from the electoral register, but supplemented using council data (such as library cards or parking fines) or through neighbours informing council officers of people's details. The use of computers was also called into question. They were expensive pieces of equipment in the late 1980s, and the idea of a council keeping a record of their citizens and taxing them merely for existing struck some as perverse.

The use of the electoral roll to identify potential payers led many to criticise the Community Charge as being a tax on the right to vote. But some Tories brushed this off. Sir Hugh Rossi, the MP for Hornsey and Wood Green, for one welcomed the linking of taxation with representation, arguing that voting and paying taxes were both civic duties, so why not combine the two?[39] The Shadow Environment Secretary, Dr John Cunningham, denounced linking the electoral roll to taxation as 'abhorrent in a democratic society', declaring 'unequivocally that if any such system were to be introduced, it would be abolished by the next Labour Government!' His opposite number on the government benches Patrick Jenkins mockingly replied: 'It is typical of the Labour Party to promise to abolish things before they know what they are.'[40]

The Scotland rates revaluation

Initially the government proposal was for a twin-track approach called 'dual-running', retaining the rates but gradually phasing them out over time, with the Community Charge increasing incrementally annually. Certainly sceptics like Lawson as well as top civil servants were planning on such a transition phase, possibly bringing the Community Charge in over four to ten years, in the first year charging people only £50. The initial proposal was for the Poll Tax to entirely replace the rates by the year 2000.

But the best laid plans of mice and men gang aft a-gley, as the poet Robbie Burns famously wrote. After years of prevaricating, the government conducted a rates revaluation in Scotland in 1986. The way it was calculated meant that middle-class homeowners in particular lost out, causing serious worries for the Conservatives about a potential hit on their voting base. Some rate-payers found their bill increased by an eye-watering 300 per cent. In more affluent parts of Edinburgh the rates bill for a four-bedroom detached bungalow rose from £1,600 to £2,347.[41] Sir James Goold, the chairman of the Conservative Party in Scotland, visited Thatcher to warn her of 'the fury that had broken out north of the border'.[42] This led to chaos for the Conservatives and forced them to accelerate their plans.

While the Tory vote in the 1987 general election held up in England, a further nail was driven into the Conservative coffin north of Hadrian's Wall. The Conservatives were reduced from 21 MPs in 1979 to only ten by 1987, causing serious consternation throughout the party with Tory MPs in marginal English and Welsh seats sweating about rates increases that might in turn see their voters desert them. If the Scots could be that vengeful, what would happen in the Home Counties?

This spurred some on to consider alternatives. A growing number of MPs were now backing the Community Charge, and the debate increasingly moved from whether it was a good idea to how quickly it could be implemented. The initial thinking was that it entailed such a shift in financial arrangements that a transition period was preferable. Had the transition phase policy been adopted it is very likely that the Anti-Poll Tax movement would have been neutralised – certainly it would not have had the same intensity. People tend to acclimatise and adapt to changes over time. What made the difference in 1989/90 was the sudden impact of the new costs hitting so many people at once.

By mid-1987 only a minority of hard-line Thatcherites like Ridley were pushing for immediate implementation, with most still favouring a dual-running system. All of that changed at the Tory Party conference later that year, when the ex-MP for Aberdeen South (who had just lost his seat), Gerry Malone, made a passionate speech claiming that the atrocious rates system was to blame for his loss, cursing the old financial arrangements, and calling on the party to consider immediate alternatives: 'We've had the courage to take on the challenge. Let's do it properly. Let's do it as soon as we can.'[43] This appealed to a number of Tory MPs who initially believed their own propaganda that the Community Charge would be cheaper. Thatcher in particular loved the speech. Lawson and his allies got wind that the mood was shifting on the dual-running phase, leaving them furious and paranoid that Ridley had put Malone up to it, a charge he strenuously denied. After the conference a special Cabinet was convened to discuss scrapping the dual-track approach and just going ahead with a 'big bang', a strategy approved by Ridley and Michael Howard. Now the Community Charge in all of its terrible wretched glory would come down upon the Scots within two years.

The 'loony left'

Politically, the Poll Tax has to be seen in the context of the war on the so-called 'loony left' councils in the 1980s. Thatcher's unrelenting battle against 'Town Hall Socialism' was rooted in her desire to destroy progressive politics wherever she could find it. It was also premised on an understanding that the municipalities were some of the last redoubts of the Labour left, as Neil Kinnock's attempt to purge the Labour Party of radical dissenting voices was in full swing by the late 1980s. Thatcher's approach was described as 'a war against local government',[44] one that had to be fought to 'decontaminate the middle classes of collectivism and socialism, while persuading aspirational workers that restoring small government and free markets would create the conditions in which they, and their families, could "get on"'.[45]

By the end of the decade Thatcher's war had been largely successful. Over 40 pieces of legislation had been passed since 1979 specifically targeting the financial and political autonomy of local government. The Greater London Council, run by Ken Livingstone and John McDonnell, had been abolished in 1986. The left-run Independent London Education Authority (ILEA), responsible for most of the schools in London, was in the process of being abolished. The municipal left – including people like Derek Hatton in Liverpool, Margaret Hodge in Islington, David Blunkett in Sheffield and Ted Knight in Lambeth – were all either out of power or had been co-opted by the Labour Party right into the new realism. This isn't to say there were no left-wing Labour councillors in power, but they did not have the backing of their national party and were easy prey for right-wing tabloid onslaughts.

The Conservatives' party political broadcast designed to sell the Poll Tax to the electorate in 1988 is instructive in this context. It deployed the analogy of local government finances being equivalent to the water in a pot of tea. A large part of the water, the broadcast explains, comes from national taxes, some from a national tax on businesses (which left-wing Labour councils could 'no longer squeeze' locally), while the remaining

25 per cent of council funding will come from the Community Charge. At this point the tea pot is full – so what do councils now decide to spend it on? The analogy has the tea pot being poured into cups labelled 'Sport and Leisure', 'Housing' and 'Dustman'. Spending on such things would lead to a Poll Tax of only £178 per person – cheaper than the rates in many places. 'However', warns the stern voiceover, 'If your council wastes money on extravagant services it will have to ask for an even bigger Community Charge.' The tea is then frivolously poured into cups labelled 'Police Monitoring', 'Nuclear Free Zone', 'Foreign Travel', 'Gay Seminars', 'Over-Manning'. Just to drive the point home, the camera zooms in on the Gay Seminar cup. At this point the total sum in the corner of the screen is rocketing up: £280, £300, £320.

The message is clear: pensioners, people on low incomes and lone parents should be appalled at local councils spending money on services for LGBT people. In the Conservative mindset of the time it was impossible to imagine a gay pensioner or a lesbian single parent. After all, for many with such a mindset, homosexuality was a personal perversion, something that should be kept behind closed doors, not something for local authorities to be 'promoting' – and indeed this was the same year that the notorious Section 28 was introduced, outlawing the promotion of homosexuality. It is impossible, then, to understand the Poll Tax without seeing it as part of the wider culture wars of the 1980s. When it came to the fight to remove LGBT issues from public life the Conservatives lost that battle so spectacularly that they were forced into a volte face and legalised same-sex marriage in 2013.

The Conservative manifesto for the 1987 general election proposed that the rates system be entirely scrapped and replaced by 'a fairer Community Charge. This will be a fixed rate charge for local services paid by those over the age of 18, except the mentally ill and elderly people living in homes and hospitals.'[46] The Community Charge was depicted as a way of creating 'fairness', since everyone (with few exceptions) would pay the same amount.[47] Labour's defeat and Thatcher's third victory convinced the Tory establishment that people were as aggrieved with the rating system as much as the party rank and file were, and that the new financial arrangement would enjoy general support. This sense of complacency was reinforced by the 1988 local elections, in which the Conservatives managed to hold their ground – securing 39 per cent of the popular vote, as against Labour's 38 per cent. Labour gained eight councils, the Conservatives seven. Almost a score draw. Certainly the result did not cause the Tories to have any thoughts about changing course.

By this stage, the Poll Tax was being relished by some passionate right-wingers. In 1988 Eric Pickles led the Conservatives to victory in Bradford, becoming the only inner-city council to be run by the Tories, though they only had a majority of only one. Pickles immediately announced cuts worth £5 million, aiming to shed 9,000 jobs and privatise 15 elderly care homes as well as three sports centres and the city's swimming pool. 'We'll have the lowest Poll Tax in Britain', he boasted.[48]

To deliver her flagship policy, Thatcher replaced Patrick Jenkin with Nicholas Ridley as Secretary of State for the Environment. Ridley was a chain-smoking public school boy, a Thatcherite loyalist, and as contemptuous as the Prime Minister was of the liberal Tories, the 'wets'. As Minister for Transport he had stock-piled coal prior to the miners' strike to ensure there was no repeat of the three-day week that had blighted Ted Heath. Ridley was tasked with forcing the new tax through Parliament in the face of Labour opposition. But for the Thatcherites Labour was not the main problem – it was people like Heseltine and Ted Heath, who posed the danger of whipping up opposition from the Tory backbenches. Ridley headed off the opposition at the pass by announcing that there would be greater scope for rebates to prevent too many negative headlines. The rebate system, known as Community Charge Benefit, was capped at 80 per cent of the overall cost, so, unlike under the old system, the poorest still ended up having to contribute. Aware of the primary criticism, the government made it clear that people on low incomes would pay only 20 per cent of the tax, and claimed that pensioners and lone parents would also be 'better off' under the Community Charge. This was enough for some opponents, and the party whips used the usual mix of cajoling, bullying and threats for the rest. The potential for a backbench revolt fizzled out, with only 17 voting against the legislation at the second reading, and with 15 abstaining. An amendment from Michael Mates, which aimed to dilute the most iniquitous aspects of the tax by introducing a banding based on ability to pay, was also defeated. Neither Thatcher nor the Treasury liked it.

The threat of a revolt in the Lords followed, with an amendment along the lines of what Mates had proposed in the Commons, this time put forward by an old grouse-moor buffer named Sir Tufton Beamish. William Whitelaw, who had just had a minor stroke, was wheeled out to plead with the Tory Lords for loyalty. A number of mostly absent peers were also whipped to appear in the chamber, producing the largest turnout since the constitutional fight over Lloyd George's budget in 1911.[49]

Ian Aitken, the *Guardian's* political correspondent, was notably cautious about the appearance of near total support for the Poll Tax as a proposal among Tory MPs: 'the truth about the poll tax is that, far from there being only 17 MPs opposed to the idea, it would be very difficult to muster 17 Tory MPs who genuinely and unequivocally support it'.[50]

With the Community Charge now agreed, and the machine being put in place to implement it, the government was taking a huge gamble. It was noted at the time that only one other country in the world had a similar tax, Papua New Guinea, and their government was on the verge of abolishing it.[51] Nigeria had also recently abolished their poll tax. It had been imposed on both countries when they were British colonies. The government tried to argue that Japan also had a poll tax for local finance, but on closer inspection it was revealed that it was part of a property tax and only accounted for 1 per cent of local government funding (about £20 a year in 1990 prices).[52] The other recent poll taxes in the modern world had been imposed in the southern states of the USA as a means of disenfranchising blacks, alongside qualifications such as literacy and understanding the constitution.[53]

Could the Tories pull off what seemed so impossible in the modern age? One academic, writing in 1988, declared that 'no tax has ever been more unpopular than the local rates'.[54] As we shall see, the Conservatives were about to put that claim to the test.

3
Scotland

'The burden should fall, not heavily on the few, but fairly on the many.'
Margaret Thatcher

It still remains a source of great anger and anti-Tory sentiment in Scotland that Thatcher trialled the Community Charge there. The Tories' reasoning was that they were helping the people of Scotland who had complained about their rates being too high since the revaluation. They believed the tax would be cheaper than the rates for a lot of people. After all, Ridley's figure – publicised in the Poll Tax party political broadcast – explicitly stated that the Community Charge would be on average only £178 per person. As Secretary of State for Scotland, George Younger ruthlessly pursued the introduction of the tax, overriding the objections of Lawson and others.

The figures did not convince many Scottish people, who implicitly did not trust the Tories and believed the tax was a punishment of the largely Labour-voting Scottish working class. Certainly they were made to feel like guinea pigs stuck in the wheels of local bureaucracy,[1] confined in a cage constructed for them by Tory MPs from the shires. Ironically, Thatcher recorded in her memoirs how she thought introducing the tax in Scotland first was doing the Scots a favour, as it was undoing the painful rates re-evaluation from 1985.[2] As David Torrance notes, 'The Prime Minister had made the crucial mistake of confusing a disgruntled minority of Scottish Tory rate payers with Scots in general.'[3]

Regardless of how Thatcher recorded her intentions, official papers released in 2014 indicated that Scotland was indeed seen by at least some English Tories as a testing ground. A memo from the young Dorset MP Oliver Letwin to Thatcher recommended using 'the Scots as a trail-blazer for the real thing'.[4] It was left to the Scottish to wonder what the practical difference was between being a trail-blazer and a guinea pig. Any potential public opposition was dismissed by leading Tories, claiming it would only amount to a 'nine-day wonder' – their contemptuous reference to the failed 1926 general strike.

Scotland had already suffered under the economic policies of the 1980s. Nearly a million workers in Scotland were paid below any kind of living wage calculations. The country had undergone widespread deindustrialisation, with as many as 20,000 manufacturing jobs lost year on year since the start of the decade. Glasgow alone had lost 65,000 well-paid manufacturing jobs. This had a knock-on effect on the unions, who had been in a state of free fall since the miners' strike, and the Scottish TUC (STUC) was led by people who seemed utterly bereft of strategy beyond merely ensuring survival.

At the same time the Labour Party itself was undergoing some deep and fundamental changes. Reeling from the battering Labour took at the 1983 general election and the growing hegemony of New Right ideology, Neil Kinnock was leading a headlong rush to the right in his attempt to make Labour electable again. A significant part of the Kinnock mantra for any historical analysis of the Poll Tax was his assertion that Labour could either be a party of protest or a party of power – either a party dominated by the left or one controlled by sensible moderates who could win government. The main argument from the right of the party was that the left was obsessed with 'gesture politics', with showmanship and posturing which was costing precious votes. By the time the Poll Tax was being introduced the Labour leadership was in no mood to countenance advocating any direct action opposition. This dynamic tension and split between the strategies of the leadership and the rank and file would become a key feature of the Anti-Poll Tax campaign.

The wider decline of parts of the traditional left certainly had an impact on how the movement evolved. Historically, the more radical wing of the trade unions in Britain had been heavily influenced by the Communist Party of Great Britain. However, despite the influence that parts of the official Communist movement had on the Labour leadership, the actual CPGB played no serious leading role in the fight to stop the tax. At the CPGB conference in 1989 they adopted the views of the editorial board of *Marxism Today*, accepting 'the end of the old forms of industrial and class conflict',[5] and began to finally address the issues of LGBT, feminist and environmental politics. But for the CPGB the turn came too late. After over a decade of deep internal divisions they were too exhausted and divided to play any serious role in the Anti-Poll Tax movement, conceding ground to the Trotskyists and Anarchists. Intellectuals like Eric Hobsbawm and the journal *Marxism Today* provided a lot of intellectual ballast for Labour's new orientation under Kinnock.

But it was not just the radical left that filled the space being created through the realignment of politics. As the working class and its traditional organisations had taken a battering, this created a political gap that was inevitably filled by a rise in Scottish nationalism. While in England and Wales the left succeeded to a degree in making the Poll Tax about class, and questioned its legitimacy on grounds of the moral economy for that very reason, the fight against the Community Charge in Scotland had the additional dimension of the national question. As Richard Bellamy noted, the economic devastation of the Thatcher era had the result of impoverishing and marginalising around 10 per cent of the population, and 'the fact that this exclusion of a minority from national prosperity was as much territorial as class or sectorally based had the additional effect in Scotland of strengthening the sense of national distinctiveness, at least in political if not necessarily cultural terms.'[6]

For the propagandists in the Scottish National Party the tax being introduced to Scotland first was a gift from heaven. What clearer example of anti-Scottish reaction from the English rulers in Westminster could you hope to see? This was a tax designed to provide succour for Tory voters in the south-east and make working-class Scottish people pay the price. The SNP were quick to point out how few Tory MPs there were in Scotland and that Thatcher had no mandate to impose her tax on the people north of the border. Politically, the SNP saw the tax as a break with Article 18 of the 1707 Treaty of Union which stipulates that no tax may be levied on one part of the kingdom and not another.

Labour hoped to steer the argument from an anti-English one that would only strengthen the SNP into safer, more social democratic channels. Nevertheless the Scottish Labour MPs were not averse to using the argument around Scottish identity and distinctiveness as a stick to beat the tax with, with John Maxton, for example, describing it as a policy 'imposed in Scotland by a government with no mandate to do so and one that the Scottish people have so clearly rejected.'[7] However, in the 1987 general election Labour had barely mentioned the Community Charge, despite the fact that it was already the subject of many press column inches, workplace talk and pub chatter up and down the country.

Labour's efforts were undermined by the fact the SNP was on a left trajectory at the time, capitalising on Labour's march to the right and the consequent disillusion of some of its activist base. The SNP was calling for the renationalisation of privatised industries, a minimum wage and a mass council house building programme. This left-flanking of Labour was only exceeded by Militant, with thousands of members across the country and considerable influence in Labour Party Young Socialists, snapping at the heels of the party leadership. Although its editorial board had been expelled in the early 1980s and it had come under concerted criticism and attack over its activities on Liverpool City Council, Militant still enjoyed considerable support across the Labour grassroots. At a mass rally held in 1985 around 10,000 people had turned out to hear their leader Ted Grant speak.

But both the SNP and Labour faced a problem. In Scotland the Tories controlled only three small district councils, which meant the Tory tax would have to be implemented on the ground by non-Tory politicians. While the SNP and Labour opposed the tax, though neither yet had a credible alternative to it, they would be supposed to implement it through their control of local councils. The contradictions between the national positioning and the local practicalities of implementation were immense. Labour left activists knew that their party would be a battleground when it came to a strategy of opposition to the Poll Tax. The debates in the party in the run up to rate capping had seen general support for a position of non-compliance and outright opposition, but the Labour leadership had pulled back, urging councillors to not go too far and that it was better to be in power and implement cuts than not – the infamous 'dented shield' approach. As for the SNP, their councillors were usually on the right of the party. They controlled Angus District Council, which was the first to (voluntarily) cooperate with the tax.[8] But in Grampian Regional Council the SNP councillors refused to appoint sheriff officers to collect any debts causing a breakdown in their coalition with the local Liberal Democrats.

It may have seemed at first glance that the balance of forces were against stopping the Poll Tax in Scotland, as the organisations that people would have looked to in order to resist the tax were either exhausted or unwilling to take a stand. It was in this space that people had to consider alternative organisations and ways of fighting.

Many Scottish delegates to the Labour Party conference in Brighton in 1987 spoke passionately about their opposition to the tax, calling on Labour to take direct action against it. The argument was continued at the Scottish Local Government conference a month later in Stirling. The result of these debates was the 'Stop It' campaign.

Stop It was a classic Labour Party style campaign, a kind of concession to the virtue of opposition and direct action but organised along very safe, controlled lines. Chaired by the unimaginative committee man Brian Wilson, the campaign urged people to fill in their registration forms but make several queries about them, essentially to slow down the introduction of the tax. Stop It also urged councils not to collect the tax, but there was no serious effort put into actually coordinating councillors or officers to make that happen. The campaign focused on legal action, trying to secure injunctions against the tax as the registration forms were sent out with material that it was argued was illegal due to breaches of privacy. The secretary of Stop It was John Rafferty, who spoke in very unsympathetic terms of the 'fashionable' and 'chic' non-payment campaign – for him as a trade unionist non-payment meant less money for local government which in turn meant job losses for hard-working council employees. It was this narrow industrial view which dogged British trade unionism and rendered it ultimately largely irrelevant in the wider fight against the Poll Tax.

Labour leaders wanted to orientate the strategy around stopping the tax before it was introduced, knowing that once it was they would feel compelled to implement the law. There were clashes with those calling for a mass tax-refuser movement. The right of the party insisted that such a proposal was too radical, potentially too explosive. They did not want a mass movement; they wanted to apply political and moral pressure on the Tories to stop the tax before it got off the ground. As Anti-Poll Tax activist Danny Burns pointed out, given the timid opposition from Labour to the GLC abolition and rate capping (with the exception of Lambeth and Liverpool), this was 'extremely naive'.[9] For Burns the question was would the movement be one of mere protest before the inevitable defeat, or a prolonged resistance that aimed to win?

And it was not just Labour who were unwilling to countenance more radical opposition. The Stop It campaign was also backed by the Communist Party of Great Britain, who saw in it the strategy of the Popular Front that they had advocated since the 1930s. The Popular Front united communists with liberals, social democrats, capitalists and the church to oppose fascism, and was specifically geared to amplifying the voice of the 'progressive' establishment rather than mobilising radical working-class forces. Such was the nature of the Stop It campaign for the CPGB – an attempt to unite the liberals and the left against the Conservatives.

The CPGB had been going through some torturous internal debates which were only deepened and exacerbated by the collapse of the Berlin Wall and the end of 'actually existing socialism' in the USSR. *Marxism Today*, their theoretical magazine, had become associated with the shift to the right in the Labour movement. Its writers praised Kinnock's efforts to purge the 'ultra-left' and create a disciplined party, while simultaneously lamenting the electoralism of Labour which led to so much 'absenteeism and inertia'.[10] They defined the Poll Tax campaign as a Popular Front, involving a cross-class alliance, before criticising the entire basis of how it was organised, describing it as 'incipiently totalitarian, because it reduces all interests to a single slogan, and subordinates all interests to the good of whichever party pulls off the popular front'. Instead they argued that the movement should learn from Live Aid and Comic Relief because they were plural and based on a concept of 'service'. For *Marxism Today*, the 'can't pay won't pay' slogan was totalitarian and divisive – what if you were still going to pay the tax but wanted to oppose it in your own way? Their appeal for a plurality of tactics was in reality a call to water down the movement and legitimise paying the tax as long as people wore a badge opposing it, much like people wore red noses for Comic Relief.

The resistance emerges

Meanwhile, away from the mass institutions of organised labour, another movement was brewing. The acorn from which the mass tax-refuser campaign grew was the small Workers' Party of Scotland, who organised meetings across Glasgow in the spring of 1987. They launched a front called the Anti-Poll Tax Union and produced a pamphlet titled 'The Poll Tax Nightmare'. Anti-Poll Tax Unions, based on going door to door, collecting donations and pledges not to pay the tax, were launched in Maryhill and then Leith. Others were launched over the summer and by the autumn of 1987 there was a call put out for coordination to sabotage the implementation of the tax. This was around the same time that Labour launched the 'Stop It' campaign – a different strategy resting on a different approach to politics.

Within a few short months the essential basis of the Anti-Poll Tax Unions (APTUs) was established and the concept of refusing the tax was gaining ground. This allowed groups like Community Resistance Against the Poll Tax (who mischievously delighted in referring to their initials – CRAPT), rooted in concepts of self-organisation and anti-authoritarianism, to gain a considerable presence in the movement. As Burns explained: 'they took political inspiration from anarchist and autonomist direct action in Spain and Italy, self-organisation charac-terised by squatters in London, Berlin and Amsterdam and the 1968 uprising in France'.[11]

Groups such as these are usually a tiny political force, but during a mass movement their organisational methods and arguments can reach an audience of thousands and win popular support. In avoiding a direct confrontation when it was clear that the tax would require one, the official Labour movement had left a gap which created new opportuni-ties, as the anarchist newspaper *Class War* noted: 'the pathetic Labour Party response to the tax in Scotland has gone a long way to increasing support for types of action that are directly effective, rather than waiting around for the politicians to get off their arses and do something'.[12]

Militant was initially cautious, at first critically backing the Stop It campaign from a distance. But when one of their councillors joined their local Anti-Poll Tax group they quickly became convinced of the non-payment campaign, and swung into enthusiastic support. This decision, while crucial for actually stopping the tax, would in the long term see Militant decisively break from Labour and end their decades-long strategy of 'entryism' into the party. For the time being, however, they hoped to remain within Labour and push the more radical strategy of sabotaging the implementation of the tax, despite the growing anger of the Labour right. A specially convened conference of Militant in April 1988, held in Scotland, hammered out the non-payment strategy. After that, the group's leader, Ted Grant, spoke at Militant meetings across the country and their three MPs, Terry Fields, Pat Wall and Dave Nellist, issued public statements in support of non-payment. Militant's position could be summed up in the words of Max Neil, a 22-year-old Militant organiser in Lancashire: 'we are calling on Labour and the unions to fight the Poll Tax under the slogan: "It is better to break the law than break the poor." We will not mince words. Labour claims to represent the very people who cannot afford the Poll Tax.'[13]

The dynamic campaign from below ruffled some feathers. It meant that even the timid Stop It campaign became too much for some people. Behind Stop It lurked the hydra of radicalism, potentially opening the door to more revolutionary voices and forces that would destabilise the comfortable new realism of the labour movement. Less than a year after

Stop It was launched there was a special Scottish Labour conference in March 1988 at which the right of the party sought to shut down a campaign which they increasingly saw as dangerous and irresponsible. The Scottish Labour leader Donald Dewar – an inveterate constitutionalist by nature – wanted to end the debates around extra-parliamentary action for good. He argued that Labour had to facilitate the Poll Tax even if it opposed it, on the basis that a party aspiring to government cannot 'afford selective amnesia when it comes to the law of the land. That would be to sacrifice its credibility to the vast majority of electors.'[14] Labour's essential message became 'must pay, will pay'. This is why in their local political messaging – including newsletters – Labour mainly attacked the Poll Tax as a 'mistake' and 'wasteful'. They sought to capture the middle ground and provide a 'reasonable opposition' to the Tory Tax, but in doing so they singularly failed to grasp the radical and deep-seated nature of the opposition to it.

In the initial public meetings, the Labour policy was causing some consternation among its voters. If the party was against the tax then why were Labour-run councils hassling tenants with registration forms? Some on the Labour left pushed for the party to mount a more determined opposition. Clearly Militant were doing so, but there were also others across the party who were keen to see Labour take a tougher stand. James McVicar, a Glasgow Councillor, issued a passionate call to arms: 'the Poll Tax represents the most regressive and vicious anti-working class law that any government in this country has ever attempted to introduce … Are we going to provide the leadership that our class demands? Are we going to provide a serious campaign of non-payment of the Tory Poll Tax, embracing the power of this mighty Labour movement, the Labour Party and the trade unions, with all the force and bludgeon that can stop Thatcher's Poll Tax?'[15]

But their reaction saw an equal and more powerful reaction. Peter Russell, a close ally of the Glasgow Council leaders Jean McFadden and Pat Lally, led the charge against the growing mood of resistance in Labour. He criticised the Stop It campaign from the right, arguing that the introduction of the Poll Tax was inevitable. All Labour could do was go along for the ride, point out its iniquities and argue that it might repeal it if it won power at the next election. A lot of these arguments were coming from the Kinnock wing of the party, desperate to move into a more mainstream position as the 'party of government-in-waiting'.

This had an impact on the Scottish TUC, who were already beginning to feel the pressure from the rank and file. The STUC General Secretary told 300 workers in Glasgow that they could not have a one-day strike against the tax, but they could have a 15-minute work stoppage. By the time the STUC week of action from 10–17 September came around, leaflets were advertising an 11-minute strike (as it was the '11th hour' to halt the tax).[16] Even 11 minutes was too much for some. When the STUC bulletin was republished by the Scottish teachers union, the EIS, they removed the reference to the 11-minute strike entirely.

At the Scottish Labour Party recall conference, the non-payment motion was defeated by 512,000 to 225,000. The substantive motion, passed with the bloc votes of the trade unions, argued that Labour should be sympathetic to those who *couldn't* pay but should avoid illegality. The overall message was clear though: if you could pay your poll tax then you should. Only delegates from the Transport and General Workers' Union (TGWU) and the National Communications Union (NCU) joined with the left CLP delegates to support non-implementation. Tom Connor from TGWU warned the delegates that: 'If we suggest the Scottish Labour Party turns its back on the people of Scotland, they will never forgive us.'[17] Right-wing delegates outside were heckled by campaigners who saw their policy as a betrayal by the party. The Scottish Executive also voted by 17 votes to 13 to oppose non-payment, leading to a rift with several Scottish Labour MPs who wanted a more intransigent approach – including Dick Douglas, who resigned as spokesperson for the Scottish Labour MPs in anger at the right's undermining of non-payment.

The same month that Labour collapsed on the question of resistance, the SNP's annual conference passed a motion of support for mass non-payment and set out to recruit 100,000 people to their cause. The SNP had seen an opportunity to out-flank Labour and seized it with both hands. Support for non-payment hovered around 40 per cent in the polls, though naturally fewer people were willing to actually commit to non-payment themselves.[18] Nevertheless the SNP was able to capture a mood of opposition in the face of Labour's equivocation.

Govan by-election

As the political forces lined up their positions on the Community Charge, there was a by-election held in Govan in November of 1988 where the SNP and Labour could test their stance with the electorate.

The by-election proved to be a total disaster for Labour. Their candidate was a well-meaning trade unionist, Bob Gillespie, a solid and reliable man of the old school who had publicly come out to say he wouldn't pay the tax, only to be publicly rebuked by his own party. The Labour media unit at the time was run by Peter Mandelson, and his team were in no mood to court any whiff of radicalism. Gillespie was totally outmatched by an ex-Labour MP turned SNP firebrand Jim Spillars. Spillars was not only an excellent orator but was also steadfast in his argument for non-payment, backed up by his party. Labour MP Dennis Canavan summed up the problem for Labour: 'Spillars would be telling the voters: "don't pay!" whereas Labour would be telling the voters: Stump up!' The election was a rout: Labour had it's 19,509 majority overturned to see the SNP comfortably take the seat with a majority of 3,554.

This stunning defeat sent shock waves through Labour. At heart they had seemed unable to win the argument that their party could best defend the Scots from Thatcherism. This was bound up with a general sense of Scottish decline, of all the old certainties falling away. The SNP was offering something new and radical; Labour was asking the Scottish people to wait until 1992 to see any change.

There were lots of lessons to be drawn from the Govan debacle but Labour drew only one – it convinced Kinnock and his spin-doctor Mandelson to tighten the screws on prospective parliamentary candidate selections and ensure that media savvy and articulate moderates got through, not old trade unionists who did not 'play well' in the media. Jim Sillars later said: 'The Govan result ended years in which the SNP was utterly despised by most of the Scottish population, who blamed it for allowing Thatcher's government to get in. Between 1979 and 1988, life for members of the SNP was most unpleasant on the doorstep. You were told in no uncertain fashion to F-off. Simple as that. The Poll Tax helped in that the SNP was seen to be active, alive and on the side of the people. The Govan by-election result seemed to cure that deep animosity towards the SNP.'[19]

The Committee of 100

The Stop It campaign's final gasp was the delivery of a 300,000-strong petition to 10 Downing Street on 1 February 1989. The delegation, made up of senior trade unionists and clergy, had done all that they could within the limits that they set themselves. The petition had been a serious effort by the forces of civil society but it went the way of most petitions to governments – nowhere.

After Stop It was stopped, a new campaign was launched, one that specifically aimed to move the opposition away from mass forces and towards symbolic gesture politics by a small number of establishment people. The Committee of One Hundred Leading Scots – otherwise known as the Committee of 100 – was proposed by the Labour MP Iain Gray. The idea was to form a civil society opposition of pillars of the community who would publicly refuse to pay the tax as a point of principle. It was based on the Committee of 100 that Bertrand Russell had set up as a split from CND in 1960, proposing more consistent direct action against nuclear weapons instead of just the usual peaceful marches. As such, the 1987 Committee of 100 (initially only 50 people) harked back to the historical glory of an earlier movement which had ostensibly appeared to be more radical and anti-establishment, even though they were thoroughly establishment themselves. They intended to throw the gauntlet down to the Conservatives – would you imprison MPs, bishops and university academics? They would refuse to pay the tax, pay their old rates into a bank account, and use the interest to help pay costs for the campaign. In contrast to the Anti-Poll Tax Unions' slogan 'can't pay, won't pay', the Committee of 100 leading lights of Scottish civil society stood for 'can pay, won't pay'.

Many grassroots activists were not impressed with these strategies or the lukewarm position of many in the Labour Party establishment. Labour's MPs in Scotland were labelled the 'feeble fifty' by campaigners. Already the party was losing its grip on the political narrative and the nascent struggle. The only headline-grabbing act of resistance came from Ron 'Red' Brown, Labour MP for Edinburgh Leith, who grabbed the mace in the Commons and threw it on the floor, denting it. He was made to pay a fine and read out a pre-agreed statement written by the Speaker of the House. He deviated from the speech, and when called to order by the Speaker, turned on him: 'Since you know the grovelling statement, Mr Speaker, I am not going to read it out.' He was suspended for 20 days and fined.

While for some non-payment was a moral question, for others it was a case of literally not having the money to afford it. When the Scottish councils started to set their budgets around March 1989, the Poll Tax figures turned out to be far higher than civil servants had calculated. Lothian Regional Council set it at £305, Tayside at £241, Edinburgh at

£392. Ridley's £178 was starting to look like a fantasy figure at this point. In July 1989 Ridley issued a new figure, based on standing spending assessments, of £242 per head. But to achieve this would have meant massive austerity cuts across the board for local authorities. Within this contradiction lay the crucial question of a political fight by the movement to turn a key argument for the tax around by 180 degrees.

For her part, Thatcher remained implacably clear on the righteousness of the Community Charge, adamant that the very high bills would inevitably be blamed on 'grossly extravagant local authorities'.[20] When it became clear that poverty-stricken boroughs in inner London or Glasgow were inevitably going to pay more in Poll Tax than a local authority in the shires, Thatcher simply replied that the issue was one of efficiency.

With only a week to go until the tax was introduced, Campbell Christie, the General Secretary of the STUC, gave a speech in which he pledged not to pay his Poll Tax for a full three months and encouraged others to do the same to register their protest. Anarchist campaigners laughed at his position, pointing out that everyone had a three-month window in which to pay their tax anyway: 'Christie's intervention was the equivalent of announcing that you are not going to be paying your gas bill until you got the red one.'[21]

On 1 April the tax was introduced. For people in Scotland who were on low wages and had been forced to take worse employment after their well-paid manufacturing jobs had been eviscerated by government policy, the arguments about a 'fair tax where everyone paid the same' fell decidedly flat. A flat tax – even one on a council-by-council basis – is only fair if everyone is paid the same. Under capitalism, the equalisation of wages is impossible, since the essential exploitation of the workforce in pursuit of profit mitigates against any such equality. The government tried to win the argument by pointing to the rebates and discounts, claiming that this fundamentally changed the Community Charge from a flat tax to one based – to a degree – on ability to pay, making it far more progressive than even the rates were. However, even people on only £30 a week income support had to pay 20 per cent of their bill. In some inner city councils with huge tax bills that was still going to be quite literally unaffordable.

Again the concept of fairness became a central ethical-political point around which the movement understood itself in relation to the rich power-brokers in government who imposed the tax. Even the Tory Reform Group compared the tax not only to the Peasants' Revolt but also to that other great calamity of the fourteenth century, the Black Death: 'The Poll Tax is fair only in the sense that the Black Death was fair: It is indiscriminate, striking at young and old, rich and poor, employed and unemployed alike.'[22] In fact it was clearly less fair, as a number of very rich people were saving a lot of money. The Duke of Westminster's tax bill on his two estates near Chester and Lancaster fell from £11,745 to only £1,187. Appalled at how little he was paying, the Duke was gripped by such a spirit of civic mindedness that he ended up paying the Poll Tax for his tenants as well.[23] The Prince of Wales saved £10,342 a year. Lord Vestey, owner of Dewhursts the butchers, saw his local tax bill drop from £5,000 to £208. Margaret Thatcher was due to save £1,500 on her Dulwich home.

The government's own figures modelled a 34 per cent increase in local taxes for people in northern counties but a 24 per cent drop in the south-east – representing a massive windfall for their voting base and a financial punishment for Labour voters. Dudley Fishburn, the Tory MP for Kensington, wrote in his by-election leaflet in 1988 that 'the Community Charge should be little more than £122 per head'. Despite the propaganda the reality of the tax was soon to strike home. Andrew Neil, then editor of the *Sunday Times*, came to realise how iniquitous the tax was when he found out in conversation with his cleaner that she was paying more than he was.[24]

4

Debates Over Strategy

It was clear that petitions and appeals to reason were not going to work. The tax had to be broken through making it unimplementable. The slogan adopted by the movement early on was the same as that of the Poplar Rates Rebellion of 1921, when Labour councillors led by George and Minnie Lansbury had gone to prison to defend the poor of east London: 'Better to break the law than break the poor.' The same sentiment had been expressed by the rate-capping councillors of Lambeth and Liverpool in 1985 during their failed attempt to see off Thatcherite control of local government spending. The question was what specific tactics millions of people across Britain should adopt in order to beat the government's flagship policy. The debates effectively focused on three strands: non-registration, non-payment and non-collection. All three were different approaches to resistance, but all essentially broke with the logic of the unions and the Labour Party when it came to legality.

Non-registration

In the period before the tax was launched, the question for the vast majority was whether to refuse to register to pay the tax or to focus on non-payment. There were several arguments for not registering, including the concern that it was basically a national computerised database designed to keep track of everyone. Coming only a few years after 1984, this had got many people thinking of parallels with Orwell's book – the massive growth in surveillance and control seemed to be becoming a dystopian feature of the modern age. Non-registration meant that they couldn't hassle you, because they didn't know you existed. As CRAPT put it (in an ironic echo of the advice Heseltine gave to rate payers after the increase in the early 1980s): 'when you get the form, don't delay – throw it away!' Labour councils, in contrast, advised: 'Make it easy on yourself: pay by direct debit.'

But non-registration had serious consequences, and not just in terms of the money you could be fined. Non-registration meant going off grid, what Thomas Docherty referred to, negatively, as a 'strategy of disappearance'.[1] For some in the anarchist wing of the movement this was perfectly legitimate. Many of them were already living or were prepared to live lives in a broad counter-cultural movement, based on squatting, being on the 'rock and roll' (dole) and doing cash-in-hand work. For them, getting a 9–5 job with a suit and tie in the corporate 'greed is good' 1980s was not very appealing.

As *Socialist Organiser* argued, 'the only way to avoid being on the Poll Tax register is to become a non-person – not pay rates, not pay rent, not be on the electoral register, never claim housing benefit or social security, never be ill, never go to a public library or swimming bath.... Non-registration is therefore a non-starter and we should not mislead people about this.'[2] Nevertheless, it appears that thousands of people disappeared from the electoral register in Glasgow, most likely the city with the largest number of non-registrations. Malcolm Rifkind confidently declared that 99 per cent of people in Scotland had registered for the tax – which was a blatant lie. The *Guardian* reported some years later that the 'electoral register in Scotland fell more than 27,000 in 1988, bucking the previous trend of year-on-year rises. The following year, it fell a further 34,000.'[3] If this was a tax on voting then it was beginning to eat away at its own base.

To counteract the non-registration campaign councils began to employ even more devious methods to register people behind their backs. Using the Poll Tax computers they cross-referenced people according to library records and council fines, collecting data any way they could. South Manchester College handed out green registration forms with the enrolment forms for new students. As soon as they found out, the college Labour Club approached NALGO and protested, leading to the registration forms being withdrawn under pressure from the union.

Others attempted to bribe residents. Nottingham City Council offered its residents a chance to win prizes if they set up direct debit payments. First prize was a £2,000 holiday for two; second prize £500 worth of gift vouchers; third prize, two mountain bikes.

Some people used the opportunity of the registration process to goad the authorities. After a legal challenge, Austin Underwood of Amesbury was allowed to use the name Wat Tyler on his registration form after encouraging his neighbours to also register under that name.

In practice though, regardless of political motivations, a number of people did struggle with the registration forms, and there were genuine concerns that the personal questions asked about people's relationships with each other represented an invasion of privacy. The most famous victim of the attempts to register everyone was Thatcher herself. Cabinet Office papers released years later revealed that Westminster Council had sent a registration form to the 'Resident/Owner, Rooms First Floor, 10 Downing Street, London, W1 9MN'. The Cabinet Office complained that it was 'most inappropriate' to issue a single form 'asking a number of essentially personal questions' that one person would have to answer on behalf of another. The council said it was a mistake and issued two separate registration forms. When these were not returned a reminder was sent in May 1989 by Westminster Council's chief finance officer, warning of a possible penalty for non-compliance. Civil Servants hurriedly got Denis and Margaret to fill out the forms. If the Prime Minister was having trouble, many others across the country, including the elderly and infirm, were no doubt having trouble too.

Non-collection

Non-collection was the most difficult case to make, because it meant mass-organised breaking of the law by either trade unions or councils. Either could have led to potentially explosive consequences as it would have frustrated the legal apparatus of the tax at the very core of the machine. Having councils refuse to implement a law would indicate a fracture within the state machinery, something normally only seen in a period of great political upheaval or even a revolution.

Was there a chance of organised resistance from the Labour councils to refuse to implement the tax? At the special conference of the Association of Metropolitan Authorities in 1988 it was established quite early on that there was little appetite for such a strategy. Bill Lovell, the Wealden District Council Revenue Officer, told the conference that, 'Whatever the tax, the professional local government officer will collect that tax.'[4] Ron Garner, Liverpool's Rate Accounts Manager, struck a different tone. In a city with 100,000 on housing benefit there was obviously a lot of low-income residents: 'You can't get blood out of a stone. How the heck do you go to court with someone on a minimum income?', he asked the assembled attendees. He also admitted that there were parts of Liverpool that his officers would simply refuse to go during the day, let alone at night, to register people for the Community Charge – it would be too dangerous. His comments were met with a resigned shrug.

Likewise the Labour-dominated Local Government Information Unit (David Blunkett was the president at the time) showed little support for action. At its annual conference in Newcastle the same year, the left-leaning leader of Liverpool City Council, Keva Coombes, asked delegates: 'is there any possibility left of any collective action urging people not to pay ... of going for non-implementation?' The councillors and trade union officials present were utterly sceptical. Gateshead councillor Patricia Murray replied later in the day, arguing that the priority was to mitigate the worst effects of the tax on the poorest. Calls for non-implementation were unrealistic: 'Unless every single local authority in England and Wales agreed to not pay the poll tax, we haven't got a cat in hell's chance of making the strategy succeed ... we cannot instruct our fellow councillors to break the law!'⁵ Patricia Hollis from Norwich pointed out that there was no support from the Labour front-bench for pursuing a strategy of illegality.

If the councillors and managers wouldn't act, then what about the council workforce? Essentially this meant convincing the local government unions NALGO and NUPE, who organised thousands of council workers. It also meant a fight in the civil service union CPSA, because there was collaboration between the dole office and Poll Tax collectors. There were some early successes: Lothian NALGO voted for non-cooperation with any attempt to fine people for non-payment and CPSA branches also passed motions pledging that members would not deduct money from claimant's giros. But largely speaking the trade union movement's leadership remained reluctant to get involved.

The initial view of revolutionary socialists was that the key to stopping the tax as rapidly as possible was working-class action. The pitched battles of the miners and the print workers at Wapping had ended in defeat, but those were sectional battles by one part of the class, the result of a salami tactic by the capitalists to divide and rule. The Poll Tax was a generalised offensive against the whole of the working class, this time not to destroy their unions, but to implement an irreversible shift in the balance of wealth from the poor to the wealthy.

While the revolutionary left were in favour of the APTUs, they were critical of relying on non-payment as the sole strategy, preferring to see it as a useful auxiliary to the central social forces that could bring down the government – the organised working class. In their pamphlet the Socialist Workers Party (SWP) argued that 'Even large numbers organised on a community rather than a workplace basis do not themselves possess the strength to win ... Community organisation stands in stark contrast to the power of workers organised in the workplace.' SWP activist Rob Ferguson from Greenwich NALGO argued in the bulletin of the All Britain Anti-Poll Tax Federation: 'Whilst we will undoubtedly win this campaign though mass non-payment, it we rely on that alone, we will face a long protracted battle, with services gradually diminishing and jobs remorselessly disappearing. If ... we decide as individual workplaces to take collective action, the tax can be stopped in months.'[6]

At the Scottish TUC Conference in 1988 there was significant pressure from delegates to back a non-payment campaign if Stop It failed. But there were also serious manoeuvres behind the scenes by Donald Dewar to ensure that the trade union movement did not adopt non-collection or non-payment as an official position.[7] The central overriding concern for people like Dewar – and behind him Kinnock – was Labour's electability. Any signs of radicalism had to be stamped out for the good of the party.

The radical left pushed for local council workers to stop collection and for councillors to publicly take a stand and not pay the tax, to pass local policy against it, and so on. More moderate voices from the Labour right challenged this approach, arguing that non-collection might devastate local services and that councillors shouldn't risk being personally fined (surcharged) by taking a personal stand. To some degree this was a sublimated debate between revolutionary and reformist conceptions of the scope and power of the movement. The revolutionary left saw an opportunity to develop a response from the working class within the state machinery, not merely as consumers within wider society. The idea of disrupting the workings of local government through industrial action raised the possibility of a revolutionary wedge pointed at the heart of the national state. The reformist left were entirely orientated towards non-violent mass action of people resisting an elite imposing an onerous tax. As such these arguments were also about socialist versus populist strategies.

The response from the official labour movement was disheartening. It also never really shifted during the intense three-year battle to stop the tax. In as much as it did shift it went from being tokenistic to non-existent. In November 1988 the STUC called an '11th-hour protest' to stop the tax. At 11 a.m. on 11 November, workers in Scotland were encouraged to lead an 11-minute walk out of work to register their opposition. Campaigners thought this was a joke when it was first proposed. They were even more shocked when they realised this was the limit of the trade union leaders' ambitions. Rank-and-file activists knew that an 11-minute strike, rather than being easier to pull off, was much harder. It was far easier to get support with a day of strike action enforced by a picket line outside the workplace first thing in the morning, than trying to get people to walk out mid-morning for what was in essence an extended cigarette break. Despite official endorsement from the STUC, individual unions remained non-committal over the action.

The desperate need to control and contain the resistance led to campaigns of disinformation and propaganda designed to demoralise and confuse. In December 1989, the Manchester Council leader Graham Stringer took advantage of the media blackout about the extent of the movement that had emerged in Scotland and told 1,500 local authority shop stewards that there was no mass non-payment campaign. In contrast, the left-wing deputy leader Ken Strath said he was willing to go to prison rather than pay the tax.

Alongside this there was a conscious effort to attack any radical strategy. Scottish MP Brian Wilson attended a Local Government Information Unit (a Labour-controlled body) fringe meeting at the NUPE conference and warned against illegality. He argued that attempts 'to urge people to act illegally were doomed to failure … any policy which asked people to go even further and refuse to pay the new tax, so breaking the law of the land, would be less successful and create a needless and useless diversion from the sheer oppression of the poll tax'.[8] This was echoed by Jeff Rooker, a Labour frontbench spokesman, who told the Rating and Valuation Association conference in 1988 that 'Whatever adjective is used to scorn the poll tax – and I will always prefer Michael Heseltine's "Tory Tax" – it is a legal tax; an unfair tax but legal.' The concern was that 'those same less well off citizens will simply not vote for a party advocating illegality, they have more to lose than gain from such action and they know it'.[9]

For their part, the SWP and Militant, alongside the smaller Trotskyist organisations, put forward motions at trade union conferences. They had some successes – the GMB conference in 1988 agreed that 'the union should work closely with local authorities and parliamentarians to effectively block the implementation of the Community Charge'.[10] But the bureaucracies in the unions quickly moved to quell any hint of illegality. By the 1989 GMB conference delegates voted only for a public campaign of awareness raising and asking the Labour Party to repeal the legislation. The same thing happened with the CPSA – their 1988 conference agreed to fight the Poll Tax more actively but by 1989 they had also adopted a more passive line.

In the National Union of Teachers (NUT) there was a fight between the left of the union and the National Secretary Doug McAvoy over whether to take action against local cuts that could see tens of thousands of teachers made redundant. McAvoy attacked the socialists in his union, focusing on Militant in particular, but this did not seem to convince most delegates, who passed a motion calling for industrial action if there were any job losses due to cuts associated with the Poll Tax.

In 1988 the NALGO Knowsley and Islington branches asked their national union to allow them to enter into official dispute against the creation of Community Charge collection roles. This was turned down by the union on the spurious grounds that it would only affect a small number of staff and therefore leave them somehow 'vulnerable'.[11] NALGO's president Ronnie Webster helped lead the charge against those 'ultra-left factions in many unions' calling for non-collection, arguing that NALGO members should not be 'the shock troops who will bring down the Poll Tax'.[12] The official history of NALGO notes approvingly that 'conference rejected adventurist calls for a campaign among NALGO members to urge them not to pay and to hold a ballot on non-collection of the tax'.[13] The NALGO 1989 conference rejected a motion calling on the union to back council officials in support of a campaign to not implement the tax; instead the union's position was to urge councillors not to take civil action against people refusing to pay. However, facing a growing clamour to combine the non-payment campaign with the industrial muscle of non-collection, the same conference did adopt a motion which appeared to contain some radical positions:

- that NALGO will support mass non-payment and other forms of civil disobedience if and when they become viable options as a result of the raising of public consciousness through campaigning ...
- to pressure local authorities through means appropriate to local circumstances not to pursue non-payers of the tax through civil penalties
- that branches be encouraged to ... pursue this policy by all means, including if appropriate industrial action.

The problem with this motion – as is often the case with the British labour movement – was its vagueness. It gave enough ground to rank-and-file left militants to make them believe they had made progress in forcing the union to take a tougher position, while also giving the National Executive Committee (who would have to implement any motion) enough wriggle room to find loopholes and excuses for passivity. The NEC's qualification that support for mass non-payment would only be given 'if and when they become viable options as the result of the raising of public consciousness through campaigning'[14] allowed the leadership to delay that support indefinitely. And even when there clearly was a mass non-payment campaign and huge demonstrations against the tax, NALGO's leaders still preferred to limit their opposition to propaganda. The biggest action to come out of the union's 1989 conference was £250,000 for a poster campaign around the May local elections in 1990 urging people to 'Vote NO to the Poll Tax!'

The National Union of Railwaymen instructed its delegates to the Scottish Labour Party conference to oppose all motions that referenced a non-payment campaign and support the motion from the Scottish Executive to look for alternatives. The Fire Brigade Union (FBU) motion from their 1989 conference was more sympathetic: 'In the event a mass non-payment campaign in Scotland becomes a reality our Executive Council urges the Labour Party NEC to immediately convene a special conference to initiate and lead a national campaign of non-payment.'

'One of the mistakes of perspective that we had when we started off', remembered Mick Brooks, the secretary of Ealing Anti-Poll Tax Federation, 'was that we expected more support from local authority workers in the form of strike action. And we did not get it. The reason for that is obviously betrayal by the national labour movement and the Labour Party … But if you take the average NALGO or NUPE member, if they weren't going to get national support they were snookered.'[15] As if to drive that point home, NUPE sent a circular to its branches reminding them of the 'powers of enforcement which the government have laid down and which councils are legally obliged to operate'. It was clear that the unions also expected their members to implement the tax.

Anarchist groups were also pushing for industrial action by workers. The Anarchist Workers Group urged that 'as soon as non-payers are taken to court or workers are victimised political strikes must be launched throughout the entire labour movement'.[16] They had little time, however, for putting demands on local councillors: 'Rather than lobbying councillors to persuade them to lead our cause we must simply expose their inability to play a truly significant part in our struggle.' The Anarchist Communist Federation concurred: 'the reason those council and Labour leaders have tried to wreck the fight has nothing to do with a lack of "bravery" or "guts". They haven't "sold us out" because they were never on our side to begin with. The leaders of the Labour Party and local councils have repeatedly attacked the anti-poll tax struggle, because their position and their interests dictate that they must.'[17]

Conversely, Trotskyists believed that 'putting demands' on Labour councillors would play an essential part in exposing their vacillations and inadequacies in the eyes of the working class. However, the fixation on trade union action by the Trotskyist left caused friction within the movement. For the anarchists and organisations like the Revolutionary Communist Group, the SWP were undermining the actually existing movement by waiting for mass trade union industrial action that would probably never come.

While they were active in the APTUs, Trotskyist groups were generally critical of the focus on the non-payment campaign. Socialist Organiser wrote that 'we must be clear: mass non-*payment alone will not beat the poll tax*. Community action must be used to turn the campaign into the labour movement and demand non-implementation by councils and non-cooperation from the unions.'[18] Likewise, Workers' Power were unconvinced by the dominant strategy being advocated: 'neither mass non-payment nor non-collection on their own have the power to beat the Poll Tax. If successful they will immediately come up against the courts, the police, the bailiffs. Faced with this the workers involved will need to generalise the action by calling for mass political strike action.' Since the Poll Tax represented a generalised attack on the working class, Workers' Power concluded that the call for a general strike was the appropriate response, because the other forms of resistance would inevitably come up against the force of the law (anti-union laws, councillors being surcharged, possible imprisonment or use of bailiffs for non-payment). 'It means preparing to mobilise workers in the workplace as well as on the estates so that we can use our most powerful weapon against the bosses and their government: mass strike action.'[19] A strike that struck at the flow of profit, that united people not simply as tax payers but as workers, was deemed decisive. They also called for Councils of Action based on delegates to break down sectionalism and bureaucratic control of the movement.

Militant raised the more modest proposals for a one-day general strike in Scotland on 13 September 1989, and for industrial action in response to any victimisation of workers who refused to implement the tax in any way. The strike action never materialised. Despite the bold slogans and the much heralded 'new mood' among workers – both the SWP and Workers' Power pointed to an increase in strikes in the prior 12 months as evidence that the working class was feeling more combative and coming out of the slump of recent defeats – the unions remained implacably immobile. The desire to see some kind of industrial action from workers saw *Socialist Worker* cheering on a strike by Poll Tax collection officers in Greenwich in 1990. The strike was about the extra workload created by the tax and lack of additional resources, however, not against the collection of the tax itself. The incredibly restrictive nature of Thatcher's anti-union laws meant trade unionists were forbidden from taking political action against government policies, requiring them to pitch every action in terms of narrow disputes around terms and conditions.

Arguably, the focus on the trade unions and the necessity of strike action to beat the tax underestimated the importance of social reproduction as a dimension of struggle. The fear was that an individual boycott campaign could lead to people being picked off one by one – downplaying the solidarity that was built in struggle, in communities, as hundreds of people came to know their neighbours and identified their own plight with that of others. The different reasons to boycott the tax – necessity, solidarity, politics – united and overlapped in this socially binding mechanism. The tax did not simply take effect at the point of consumption, but at the point of social reproduction due to its huge expense. As such, for many it represented a dramatic decline in the standard of living that cut right to the heart of social life. After all, could you afford to pay the Poll Tax and still feed and clothe yourself and your family, and see your friends?

Non-payment

If the organised working class could not be relied up on to mount serious resistance in the workplace, what about a generalised movement of tax resistance across society? Could the tax be stopped simply through enough people refusing to pay it? If so, then it could cause a legitimation crisis of the entire local government system – possibly even of the

Thatcher project itself – by frustrating the legal system long enough to prove the tax was unworkable.

Of course there was no reason why non-registration, non-collection and non-payment should be counterposed; they were different strategies within the wider campaign. As Lambeth Against the Poll Tax put it: 'we see registration as a first skirmish in the run up to a non-payment campaign'. But the question was which strategy it would be most effective to focus on. By the time the Community Charge notices started dropping on people's doormats the energy was behind non-payment. The right-wing ideologues who backed the Poll Tax were not phased however: 'Non-payment will collapse', predicted Douglas Mason confidently. 'People are generally law-abiding. Anyway it's hardly a great protest when you know the local authority will come along and collect the money from you.'[20]

For non-payment to succeed meant uniting people who *could* not pay with those who *would* not pay, as well as reaching out to those who were paying some of the tax but not all of it. It needed a political argument to convince people to refuse the tax alongside the many millions who were simply too poor to afford it. In this way, the social movement included both working- and middle-class activists, the unemployed alongside doctors and MPs. The media and local authorities tried to drive a wedge between the two groups, arguing that the better off were politically motivated and were cynically using the poor for their own ends. However, in many cases even those refusing to pay on principle were from lower income families who were struggling to keep up with essential payments; they refused to pay the Poll Tax because in fact they were prioritising electricity and water bills.[21]

For those who were nervous about refusing to pay anything it was recommended that they pay their tax but only at the level of the rates they had previously paid. This opened up a second crisis for the councils – the large numbers of tax-refusers were now joined by the even larger numbers of people not paying the full amount. Campaigners obviously weren't in favour of local cuts and they knew that non-payment could potentially damage local government finances, but it was hoped that local government workers in NALGO and NUPE would organise industrial action and refuse to collect the tax, which would sink it even quicker. It might also pressure councils to lobby Westminster harder for extra funding. It was Militant who first saw the potential of a mass non-payment campaign across Britain and resolutely stuck with it until the end. They had the network of activists to pull it off and were single-minded in their focus. As Rob Sewell, author of a Militant pamphlet on the emerging movement, argued: 'Mass non-payment of the Poll Tax is the *only* weapon that can defeat Thatcher.'

The arguments around non-payment had historical roots that were especially evocative for the Scottish working class. During the battles of Red Clydeside in the period during and after the First World War, the 1915 rent strikes loomed particularly large. Mainly led by working-class women whose male partners were away fighting and dying in the trenches, the campaign saw thousands refusing to pay their rent and community collective resistance to bailiffs and sheriffs. This was working-class resistance not at the point of production in factories and workplaces, but on their estates and in their homes.[22] The similarities between trade unionists on the picket lines and working-class people standing in front of homes to prevent evictions were palpable.

Campaigners knew that non-payment would bring the front line of the Poll Tax fight literally to people's front doors, as it would inevitably lead to a conflict between residents and their council which would involve police and bailiffs. In a mass social movement that is attempting to prevent something, such as a war or an unpopular domestic policy, understanding the points of actual physical resistance becomes crucial. A demonstration is just a protest and a public meeting is just a discussion, but if you attempt to disrupt the smooth operation of the machine then the question of force becomes central. The physicality of the resistance was a very important aspect of the movement, since getting involved could lead to assault by aggressive bailiffs or the police – it could mean arrest, it could mean prison. The psychology of being involved in such a movement, as opposed to a simple protest demonstration, was profound, creating a sense of determination and self-sacrifice which carried powerful political and social weight. What would you sacrifice for the cause? One hot meal? Some money? What about three months in prison? This question was posed to people pledged to non-payment.

The key obstacle to overcome was to break down any sense of isolation. One person can be intimidated into paying, but a mass movement becomes more formidable. Paying your tax is usually a solitary affair: you send a cheque or hand over cash at the town hall, or it comes out of your wages. In a time before credit cards and loans became normalised after their aggressive promotion by banks, many people had never been in serious debt and never been visited by a bailiff, so there was a risk of intimidation. People were not used to being in debt in the 1980s – it was only just becoming normalised through the massive expansion of credit and finance. Someone being in debt in a community was whispered about; a visit from the bailiffs was a sign that something had gone badly wrong. Now the bailiffs, sheriffs and police would be visiting hundreds of people.

As rank-and-file activists began to collect pledges of non-payment, 28 Labour MPs, mostly members of the Socialist Campaign Group, publicly announced they would not pay the tax. This caused serious consternation on the Labour frontbench and gave the Tories a chance to portray Labour as full of radical misfits and dangerous refuseniks. Tory minister Kenneth Baker wrote to Kinnock naming the 28 Labour MPs, castigating them for a 'campaign to promote law-breaking by non-payment of the Community Charge' and claiming that they were promoting 'disruption and disorder'. Labour's Shadow Environment Minister, Jack Cunningham, scourge of the local government Labour left in the 1980s, replied with a clear message: 'Non-payment can never, and will never, form part of the policy of our party, which believes in democracy.'[23] Despite these arguments, hundreds of thousands of people in Scotland were not listening to the Labour Party or their trade union leaders. They were voting with their feet, or rather their money, and withholding payment.

The battle lines were now drawn between those who wanted to bring the tax down and those forces that sought to implement it.

5

The Resistance Begins

Collecting the Poll Tax in Scotland presented some serious problems for the authorities. There were the huge geographical differences between rural and urban centres to contend with for starters. The areas around Aberdeen had benefited from the Thatcher era with a localised economic boom, but the rest of Scotland had not. Within cities there were pockets of deprivation and poverty where collecting any tax would be almost impossible. The urban centres, and especially the four huge Glasgow estates of Pollok, Easterhouse, Drumchapel and Castlemilk, would inevitably become the site of some resistance to the tax. These were densely packed working-class communities – many residents had jobs but many others were unemployed or in low-paid part-time work. Of the 160,000 council house tenants in Glasgow, 60 per cent were on housing benefit. The huge housing estate of Pollok in the south-west of the city became a fortress, a bastion of resistance to the tax. Posters went up in most windows announcing that the occupants would not be paying the tax. George McNeilage, who lived in Pollok and was best friends with Tommy Sheridan at the time, recalled: 'This was something new and revolutionary happening in my community.'[1]

To highlight the plight of those on benefits having to choose between eating or paying the Community Charge, campaigners organised a week-long hunger strike in George Square. Alan McCombes and Tommy Sheridan, among others, camped out in the square in central Glasgow, building a temporary tent city and organising a petition against the tax. The smell of a trolley from Greggs bakery every morning became torture for them.

In early 1989 Labour handed in its 300,000-strong petition to Downing Street urging Thatcher to halt the tax before it was rolled out. Kinnock described the Community Charge as 'fundamentally unfair, divergent from democracy, inefficient, expensive, costly and crushing.'[2] This was the general tone of Labour's opposition: it looked good on paper, and the rhetoric captured the mood of anger about how damaging the costs would be for people across Britain, but after the petition was handed in precious little else was done practically by Labour to oppose the tax.

Local APTUs in the Strathclyde region established a federation which called a protest in March 1989. This was opposed by Labour and the STUC, and the campaigners had to go it alone from the very beginning. Through door-to-door leafleting and putting up posters they got 15,000 people out on the first big march in Glasgow. They were joined by hundreds of protesters from London, who arrived on a train chartered by the campaigners. Nicknamed 'the Red Train', it set off late the evening before, running overnight to get to the protest on time. Inevitably the crowd of mainly young people on the train started drinking and partying through the night, arriving bleary-eyed the next day to join their Scottish comrades on the protest. It proved, however, that the campaign was not going to be an exclusively Scottish affair. One participant remembered: 'It was ridiculous. Madness. But it worked. The train really galvanised the campaign in London.'

The Fed

With so many local APTUs and regional federations being set up, and with the traditional organs of struggle vacating the battlefield, it made sense for a national organisation to be established to coordinate efforts. Since they had played such a leading role in Scotland, and with Tommy Sheridan in such a prominent public position there, Militant wanted to lead the campaign. They were singularly focused on non-payment as a way of stopping the tax and were increasingly suspicious of other left organisations who were pushing their separate agendas. The anarchists in particular saw the Poll Tax movement as a nascent insurrectionary force, with people challenging the state's right to tax them and snoop on them. Militant considered the anarchists to be 'petty bourgeois' forces outside of the labour movement, while the anarchists considered Militant to be essentially reformists with a pro-Labour agenda. Each accused the other of using underhand means to retain leadership positions.

This resulted in a lot of distrust among ideologically committed activists, which many new members of the movement found confusing. It also led to a great deal of manoeuvring for control. As *Socialist Outlook* described it: 'Not least of these is the top-heavy and bureaucratic nature of the All Britain Federation. Local groups and regional federations are not encouraged to participate. Information is not widely circulated. Different political views are not integrated.'[3]

The Lothian Anti-Poll Tax Federation refused the affiliation of Muirhouse Community Resistance Against the Poll Tax because there was already an APTU in that area. Muirhouse CRAPT argued that the local APTU was dominated by Militant and was not welcoming to direct-action anarchists. Similar exclusions were reported up and down the country. Several activists got the impression that Militant wanted to control the local groups, and if they could not they would split off and set up a rival group covering a similar area. The latter group would then be recognised by the Federation but the other would not. For instance, Middlesbrough Against the Poll Tax issued an open letter about the refusal of the Militant-run Stockton APTU to help them co-organise a demonstration. At the Northern region conference they were shocked when a new APTU was announced in Middlesbrough that they had never heard of before, especially as the rival group's motions were on the agenda. They were not surprised when the delegates from the new APTU turned out to be members of Militant. Some APTUs, like the one in Whitehawk, issued leaflets simply urging people to read *Militant* (GET MILITANT! GET WISE! GET STRONGER!), with no pretence at all of being part of a broader campaign.

These tensions within the campaign were largely contained because this was a genuine movement against the tax. There were enough people involved on the ground that, while Militant led and to some degree dominated, there were also broad forces involved that had the freedom to organise. There was a criticism from some that Militant tended to 'act separately, failing to coordinate with existing groups and refusing to have anything to do with tactics and strategies other than refusal to pay',[4] while some APTUs just split and got on with the campaign separately if the manoeuvring got out of hand. However, it was at the national level that the question of who was leading the movement became paramount.

At the end of 1988, a coordinating body called the National Federation of Anti-Poll Tax Groups was set up in Oxford, composed of 35 delegates from Wales and the south of England. Around the same time, the Socialist Conference in Newcastle was held, which was bigger, though not a delegate gathering. There were already splits in London over the emphasis on non-payment in the campaign, so the strain was beginning to show over tactical questions.

THE RESISTANCE BEGINS · 59

In August 1989, non-aligned APTUs in London and Avon called for a meeting to coordinate efforts across Britain, to be held on 3 September. Not willing to be out-flanked, Militant-led federations called a rival meeting to be held two days prior on 1 September. At that meeting Tommy Sheridan, Steve Nally (Lambeth), Kath Harding (Wales) and Maureen Reynolds (Manchester) volunteered to organise the 'nitty gritty' of a conference to launch an All Britain Anti Poll Tax Federation.

Around 200 activists from non-aligned local APTUs gathered on 3 September as originally planned. They were furious about Militant's manoeuvre to seize control of the initiative and gazump them by calling for a rival conference a few days before . They decided, however, against establishing a rival federation, as they did not want to split the movement. Instead, activists from this milieu launched a network called 'the 3Ds', based on the three strategies of the movement: Don't Pay, Don't Collect, Don't Implement. They produced their own newsletter and other materials that were outside the official remit of the national federation.

Despite these controversies, 2,000 delegates attended the first conference of the All Britain Anti-Poll Tax Federation (ABAPTF). The delegates represented 550 Anti-Poll Tax Unions, 547 trade union and Labour Party branches, and various community organisations. The conference was held at the Manchester Free Trade Hall in November 1989. Sheridan liked to point out that the Hall was built on the site of a mass Chartist rally in 1832, when delegates representing a quarter of a million Chartists had pledged to boycott their taxes, causing a social crisis that led to the Great Reform Act being passed by the Whig government of Earl Charles Grey.

Militant's motivation for establishing the Federation was both practical and political. It was clear that there had to be better coordination and that a political leadership was also required for the movement since its goals were to challenge a government and defeat the most vicious anti-socialist Prime Minister of the postwar era. Clearly Militant felt itself to be in a position to provide that leadership.

At the conference there was some debate about whether organisations like the SWP could affiliate. Militant drafted and pushed through a con stitution that did not allow socialist organisations to affiliate directly – they had to send delegates through the APTUs they were active in. Some queried the sense of this; after all, why could Labour Party branches affiliate when the national party was opposed to the movement, but organisations like the SWP who were implacably opposed to the tax were barred? To others in the movement it was obvious this was a move to stymy any oppositional left currents that might challenge for leadership.

Despite such wrangling, 'the Fed' (as Anti-Poll Tax campaigners called it) was launched. It provided a platform through which to focus the campaign and was the primary means for addressing the media. It was able to organise meetings in Parliament and coordinate with the Socialist Campaign Group of MPs. Sheridan and his comrades would use these opportunities to present the damning figures over non-payment to assembled Westminster journalists – right in the heart of the belly of the beast.

The same month that the Fed was set up the crossings at the Berlin Wall were suddenly opened, and Germans from the West and the East started to shake hands again. It seemed as if the world was coming alive with mass protests against hated governments, that in both the West and the East, regime change, maybe even revolutions, were possible. Perhaps even a revolution in Britain?

Challenges and opportunities

The Fed had its critics. Labour's NEC claimed that it was a simply a front for Militant Tendency. While it is true that the national structures of the Federation were dominated by Militant, the mass movement on the ground was clearly broader than any one group. However, the balance of forces in the national leadership meant that it was difficult for anyone not in Militant to propose alternative strategies. They would find their proposals simply blocked by Militant members. As a result some anarchists proposed directly twinning Scottish APTUs with others across England and Wales to bypass the Fed entirely. This idea had some purchase in a handful of local groups, but it did not provide any answers to the questions of national coordination and campaign development. Anarchists dismissed such concerns, believing the movement would spontaneously solve any problems through sheer momentum.

Activists like Danny Burns were very critical of the Fed, but Burns himself ended up being elected onto the steering committee, which, aside from him and two others, was entirely made up of Militant supporters. His view was that it was better to be on the committee to keep an eye on Militant and to try to use it to create some kind of national publication to inform and educate the different APTUs. Others were resistant to that idea, however, leaving Burns to conclude that they did not want a

Fed newspaper because Militant were determined to prioritise their own publications.

The relationship between the national Fed and the local groups was usually fairly tenuous, especially outside of the major metropoles. While there were some centrally produced materials and occasional national meetings, most local groups were left to their own devices. A plethora of badges, leaflets and posters were produced by APTUs, who also organised a lot of autonomous local actions. This gave the movement a real sense of momentum – it was not stifled by centralised control from above and the autonomous activities often meant that local newspapers were full of accounts of local people engaging in actions against the tax.[5] Despite Militant's monothematic hammering away at the non-payment strategy, there were a variety of other tactics and initiatives that could be pursued by activists on a local basis.

Down in Cornwall a separate organisation emerged of activists who did not want to be affiliated to any national organisation. They were partly led by people involved in the Revived Cornish Stannary Parliament, a Cornish separatist organisation that believed that the 1508 constitutional alignment with England did not relate to anyone working in or associated with the tin mines.[6] As such they were less inclined to any liaison with London-based organisations. The clerk of the Stannary Parliament set up a scheme whereby Cornish people could buy £1 shares in a shell company that allegedly owned the tin mines, thus absolving them of having to pay any Poll Tax, as the tax was not approved by the Stannary Parliament as required by Henry VII's Charter of Pardon of 1508. Westminster civil servants clearly viewed this dodging of the Community Charge with contempt; there were investigations for fraud, as over 1.25 million people had applied for their £1 shares by March 1990 to try and escape the tax and the money was not accounted for.[7] The bailiffs were deployed in Cornwall a lot more often than in many other parts of the country, which Fed leaders assumed was partly because the Cornish campaigners lacked the resources of the national organisation.

By late 1989, as far as the fight against the Community Charge was concerned, the Fed was the only real show in town. The other campaigns, including Stop It and the Committee of 100, had all faded away. Labour and the TUC had reneged on any responsibility to lead the movement and were actively organising against it happening. Only the Fed remained to lead the struggle.

However, its operation was relatively modest considering the scale of the movement. The radical lawyer Rudy Narayan gave the Fed office space on Stockwell Road in Brixton for a peppercorn rent. In the run up to The Demo, as many as 20 people packed into the office to undertake the various tasks that building any mass protest generates. The routine business, however, involved just two or three people, usually Steve Nally and Louise James. Nally recalled that James was picked as an office manager because 'she was competent and professional and wouldn't take sides'. The office was essentially a glorified mail-order operation, sending out leaflets and posters to regional federations and local groups. The phone rang constantly as the activists fielded media inquiries and requests from local groups. Eventually they unplugged the phone, letting it go to the answer machine to take a break from the incessant ringing.

That Christmas, millions of people across the country sat transfixed to their TVs as the people of Romania, fed up with dictatorship and a decade of austerity politics, rose up against the hated regime of Nicolae Ceaușescu and his Securitate secret police. Other protests and strikes were threatening the regimes across Eastern Europe. Thatcher had given a speech to the Conservative Party conference the previous October claiming that 'the messages on our banners in 1979 – freedom, opportunity, family, enterprise, ownership – are now inscribed on the banners in Leipzig, Budapest and even Moscow'. The right saw the uprisings as proof that liberal democratic capitalism was the order of the day, that they were heading towards the End of History, and that all the old ideological wars were over. But many on the left saw in the uprisings parallels with their fight against Thatcher, as expressions of a desire for greater freedom, more democratic rights and a chance to forge a new kind of socialism.

The drive for radical change was not shared by all however. As one dissenting Labour MP put it: 'if the working class of Romania had shown the same resolve as the Labour leaders have in fighting the Poll Tax, Ceaușescu would still be in power'.[8]

Culture wars

There were also important cultural dimensions to the movement. Gigs were organised to raise cash for local groups and spread the non-payment message, featuring bands like Kelly's Heroes, Smashing Time, The Farm and Climax Blues Band. A festival called Rock Against The Poll Tax was organised for 1 April 1989, the day the tax was to be introduced, featuring a host of left-wing bands based in Scotland, including Deacon Blue, Wet Wet Wet, Hue and Cry and Texas. Wet Wet Wet did a write up about the gig at the Usher House in Edinburgh for their annual album aimed at their largely teenage fanbase explaining why they were campaigning. Pat Kane, the lead singer of Hue and Cry, was contemplative about the relationship between celebrity and resistance – performing for working-class people who could potentially lose everything if they refused to pay: 'We were all ex-working class enough to know that the communities we came from were having a hard time, so it seemed the least we could do to associate our glamour with these struggles.'[9] A lot of the Scottish bands took to the stage a year later for the Big Day Out, as Glasgow celebrated being European City of Culture, joining the crowd in chanting 'You can stick your Poll Tax up your arse!'

Norman Cook, soon to be known by his alias Fatboy Slim, publicly refused to pay the tax, and there was a (failed) attempt to get the song 'We're Not Gonna Pay' by the Bristol-based band Axe The Tax to number one in the singles chart.

Various punk bands from anarchist circles contributed in their own uniquely lyrically proletarian way. Punk Aid released the *Smash the Poll Tax* EP featuring Danbert Nobacon from Chumbawamba and Oi Polloi thrashing out songs titled 'Axe The Tax', 'Can't Pay Won't Pay' and 'Fuck The Poll Tax'. The Cannibals also released a song titled 'Axe The Tax'. What the movement lacked in song-title originality it made up for in the sheer quantity of thrashy, post-punk anthems. Exploited released a song called 'Don't Pay The Poll Tax', with a thundering bass riff in the background, urging listeners:

Its comin' through your letter box
A sheet for you to fill in
You know you have to do it
Cause you know you just can't win
Don't pay the Poll Tax
Stick it up her arse

The playwrights Peter Arnott and Peter Mullen wrote a play called *Harmony Row*, performed by Wildcat Stage Productions, a radical Scottish theatre group, who toured it up and down the country. In Radio

4's *The Archers*, farmer Eddie Grundy came out against paying the tax as well – one of the few concessions the BBC made to the popularity of resistance against the tax.

I shot the sheriff...

Those active in the movement had to undertake the day-to-day work of dealing with illegality. They waited for their first case. The situation in Scotland was different to England and Wales. Poll Tax refusers in Scotland did not have to face possible imprisonment as their comrades south of the border did, but the local sheriffs did have significant powers. Someone in debt to the council would have a warrant issued against them and could then have their personal possessions seized and sold – known as distraint or poinding. This amounted to a public humiliation of poor people, a sight that had been used to strike fear into working-class communities in the hope of making them compliant. There was no love for the court-appointed sheriffs in working-class communities in Pollok, Leith and Cliftonville. Many struggling families had suffered the shame of their worldly possessions being dragged out onto the lawn or the front of an estate in full view of their neighbours, while sheriffs conducted warrant sales or waited for the debt to be paid.

The sheriffs had the legal right to break into a home as long as they gave enough notice of their visit. This necessitated a degree of organisation on the part of the movement at an early stage – the local APTU had to get enough people in place to block the front doors of people's homes. If they were not protected then the sheriffs would just force open the door and start to poind the goods. The councils knew, however, that warrant sales were next to useless when it came to recovering any of the money owed – on average a warrant sale only earned back 3 per cent of the debt.[10] They were clearly designed primarily to intimidate.

In early 1989 Janet McGinn – the widow of popular Scottish folk singer Matt McGinn – refused to fill out the register. Then, when the council fined her £59, she refused to pay that too. The authorities then summonsed her to court and the judge instructed sheriffs to seize goods to the value of the debt. That was on 4 July 1989, making McGinn the first person prosecuted under the law for refusing any involvement in the Community Charge.

McGinn contacted the Anti-Poll Tax Federation and on the day the sheriff was due to arrive bus loads of protesters showed up to surround her front door. She recalled how 'there was a real air of defiance and comradeship. Someone stuck a banner up outside my bedroom window saying, "God Help the Sheriff Officers Who Enter Here", which was what the Govan women had done during the First World War when the landlords were trying to increase the rents. There was singing and speeches.'[11]

The movement could draw on the resources of the unemployed. Men and women who had been thrown on the economic scrapheap due to Thatcher's economic miracle now provided a rag-tag army of volunteers to be watchers on estates, checking for the arrival of the bailiffs. On being given the alert, they would immediately call the five numbers on their phone tree, each of which would call another five and so on. Through this method large groups of bailiff busters could be gathered at short notice to stand outside the doors of the refusers to prevent distraint.

Stopping the sheriffs became a central part of the fight in Scotland because there they had the power to enter a home without permission. The call outs to stop them resulted in very little happening – most of the time the sheriffs never showed up, or drove away at speed when confronted by an angry crowd of 50 people. Campaigners often had to wait all day, which on occasion instilled boredom but on others led to a good degree of camaraderie. During the summer people had BBQs, and children played out front while their parents sat around chatting and waiting vigilantly. Physically resisting the sheriffs, however, could lead to arrest. McNeilage remembered how he had helped prevent a young woman having her property seized: 'This lassie in her '20s was broken-hearted because there was something wrong with her cervical smear and she had to see the doctor, and as she's going out the door these two bastards are wanting to get in. I got done for two assaults just because I stood between the two sheriff officers, put my hands on their shoulders and moved them away from the tenement. And I got 60 days in jail for that.'[12]

It was illegal and we knew it…

The movement also took direct action against the authorities. The energy of the campaign created space for people to be publicly radical in opposition to an unfair law imposed by an unjust government – being against the tax took hold deep in the psyche. As the leader of the Conservative Group on Strathclyde Regional Council, Fergus Clarkson, warned his party colleagues: 'when people get a taste for civil disobedience, unless it is very severely dealt with at the time, it spreads like an epidemic'.[13]

Activists got into the offices of Strathclyde Regional Council and destroyed thousands of documents relating to Poll Tax arrears. McCombes had been involved and knew the risks: 'That was heavily illegal and we knew it, but we saw it as legit because we were protecting people. We tore the files up and threw them out the window. The lane below looked like it was covered in snow.'[14]

As the campaign in Scotland was getting under way, people south of the border were looking to get organised and drawing inspiration from the tactics and strategies of the Scots. Unlike the official Scottish Labour movement, their comrades in the south hardly bothered with any initiatives like Stop It or the Committee of 100. By the time the movement was up and running the choice was between the strategy of the Labour Party – implement with regrets and wait until better days – and that of the Anti-Poll Tax Unions.

Many APTUs were either established by existing networks of friends or by people from far-left organisations. Danny Burns recounts how his APTU in Easton in Bristol began with a handful of friends calling a public meeting – 50 people showed up. They collected enough money to print 2,000 posters with 'No Poll Tax Here' emblazoned on them. After putting them through every door in the local area, they went back a week later to see who had put them up – finding around 100 in windows. Those doors they knocked on. Through these methods neighbours met neighbours and political organisations were formed.

Other APTUs emerged from existing networks built during previous campaigns. Jimmy Haddow – a Militant member in Thanet – recalled how in 1988 there had been a fight with the Tory-run council who were trying to sell their council homes off to a private company. The fight to 'save our council homes' had been partially won, helping to give local activists a sense of purpose and comradeship going into the Poll Tax campaign.

The Anti-Poll Tax movement saw the largest public meetings in living memory, especially in the south. In Grantham, Thatcher's hometown, nearly 400 people attended the launch of the local APTU. In response the district council banned them from using the leisure centre for meetings. Across the north there were meetings in small towns and even in villages too. Tony Green remembered travelling to Ulceby: 'Ulceby is a relatively small place, and was hardly a hotbed of political ferment, even in comparison to Grimsby; and yet 40 to 50 people came out to hear two unknown people who had never and never would hold political office, speak. My comrade Richard and I lingered a little too long in a nice little pub by the train station after the meeting, resulting in our missing the last train back to Grimsby and having to hitch-hike home. Eventually, when it seemed like we would have to walk the whole 19 miles or so, we were picked up by a kindly Jehovah's Witness who spent the journey trying to save our reluctant Marxist-Atheist souls.'[15] Green was active in Militant at the time, during a period of almost unsustainable levels of activity, with meetings, leafleting and canvassing being organised across the Grimsby and Cleethorpes area.

The scale of the local groups had few recent historical parallels. The miner solidarity groups during the strike of 1984-5 had been similar in that they were well-organised and nationwide, but they were largely in support of strikes elsewhere – people in London and Manchester collecting for people in Kent and Yorkshire. It was a support network for an industrial struggle. The Anti-Poll Tax Unions *were* the struggle. And they were territorially based, local, made up of neighbours and friends and sometimes family. This meant that the smear campaign tactics employed against the miners could not work in the case of the Poll Tax struggle – a largely urban campaign stretching from inner Glasgow through to Hastings. The initiative was clearly with the radical left. In his diary Tony Benn recounted attending his first Anti-Poll Tax meeting in Sheffield: 'there was a great deal of anger there, and the ultra-Left attacked people who said they would pay the tax'.[16]

Not all the APTUs were welcomed. In some places local church groups and NGOs formed Anti-Poll Tax forums which held seminars and published pamphlets on the effects of the tax on the poorest people. The forums were essentially an alliance of churches with right-wing Labour MPs and various community groups – well-meaning liberal worthies and advocates against inequality. While these forums provided very useful material on the working of the Community Charge, and sought to apply pressure on the government to amend it or even scrap it, they were not advocates of a non-payment campaign.

The establishment of an APTU in Coventry – a prominent Militant area – was met with derision by the *Coventry Evening Telegraph*. Its editorial slammed the organisation for 'being led by the political miscreants of Militant'. The newspaper was more positive towards Coventry

Against the Poll Tax, which was more of a 'vicars and the mayor' style campaign, but contemptuously concluded that 'neither [campaign] can succeed. It's too late for protest and most people are too decent to break the law.'[17]

Despite the growing momentum, the official leaders of the labour movement still resisted taking action. The TUC sent out a circular in March 1989 explaining that unions should not affiliate to any of the 'don't pay campaigns' as the official policy of both the TUC and Labour was compliance with legislation. The document, signed by TUC secretary Norman Willis, urged union members not to attend any demonstration called by Anti-Poll Tax Unions. The TUC called their own protest on 1 July 1989 in Manchester. The marchers ended up in Platt Fields, but thousands peeled off to the Capri Ballroom to hear Sheridan speak, while Willis took to the stage telling the assembled remains of the demonstration, 'I know that some of you here won't like what I'm going to say, so let's have a good boo now... 1, 2, 3 boooo...', before telling the assembled crowd they should pay their tax. People booed. After that admission of capitulation, a hired choir started defiantly singing a song about non-payment until the officials turned off their microphones.[18]

Although the campaign was strategically focused on non-payment, applying pressure to shame councillors was an important secondary front. After Labour HQ on Walworth Road had put the stick about and demanded submission from their local government representatives, most Labour councillors confined themselves to defiant but impotent anti-Tory outbursts for the newspapers, but were mostly unwilling to do anything practical for the campaign. As was often the case, the political battle raged across the letters pages of local newspapers. One recalcitrant local councillor who liked to talk left – disparagingly referred to as 'communist councillor John Peck' by his detractors – declared that in the face of the Community Charge resistance was futile: 'Gary Freeman [the secretary of Nottingham APTU] calls on me to vote against implementation of the Poll Tax. To do so would be akin to turkeys voting for Christmas. Will [they] never learn from history? Clay Cross, Liverpool and Lambeth shows the futility of an outright confrontation with the government.'[19] A Mrs Minny replied: 'He asks what of Clay Cross, Liverpool and Lambeth. I say to him, where would the Tolpuddle martyrs, the suffragettes and the East Berliners be with his cowardice leading the way?'[20]

In an attempt to ward off criticism, the Labour Party launched its own 'Poll Tax Protest', beginning in April 1989. Local branches were encouraged by the General Secretary, Larry Whitty, to organise street stalls and canvassing where 'the Poll Tax Protest will be a major focus'. The protest was described as 'a unique and exciting experiment in political campaigning'. In fact it turned out to be a damp squib, involving a handful of street stalls but mainly the usual door-to-door canvassing alongside adverts in national papers paid for by the unions.

Compared to this stale approach, the various regional federations were growing rapidly. Avon Federation had 32 groups as of October 1989 and 11 trade union affiliates. The Welsh Federation had 70 affiliates from unions, trades councils and 30 local APTUS across the country. Strathclyde Federation was massive and organized APTUs in every town.

In the early months of 1990, meetings were organised up and down England and Wales to push the line of non-payment to as many people as possible. While a hurricane was battering Eastbourne in February 1990, around 600 people gathered at a APTU meeting to hear Peter Day, the only Labour councillor in the town, extol the power of a mass non-payment campaign. The reporter at the meeting confidently confirmed that 'the possibility of fines and having property confiscated deterred no one'.[21] As the date for the launch of the tax in England and Wales drew closer, campaigners organised public burnings of their registration forms. People would gather around braziers and cheer as their neighbours and friends threw the official forms into the fire. On the Broadwater Farm Estate in London – the site of violent protests in 1985 that led to many arrests and the death of a policeman – the registration rate was only 5 per cent. Alongside these communities a few Labour councillors were also publicly refusing to pay their tax, though people were surprised by how few. In Brighton there were seven rebel councillors.[22] One of them, Jean Calder, told a meeting of the Hanover APTU: 'most of the rights of the oppressed people have been won though civil disobedience. There are things higher than the law, such as justice and love of humanity. If obedience to the law becomes a fetish then freedom and democracy disappear.'[23]

Campaigners came across people who were incredibly vulnerable, those who had suffered most under a decade of Thatcherism. Maureen Reynolds, a member of Militant and active in the APTU in Manchester, was canvassing door to door in a tower block when she came across an old man, dishevelled and nervous. He seemed almost embarrassed as he peered at her from behind his door. His flat had no floorboards, and the wallpaper was peeling off the walls. The man told her he could not pay the tax, even with the rebates. He glanced around the corridors: 'You haven't had many replies from the flats have you? But most of them are in, they're too ashamed to open their doors and frightened ... they're old too.'[24]

The battle of the council chambers

The first skirmishes in the Poll Tax fight proper came when local councils had their budget-setting meetings, at which they would decide on spending and begin the process of setting what the level of Community Charge was going to be.

Up and down the country people were preparing for action. In Lambeth the night before the budget setting meeting, a young Militant member named Andy Tullis was sitting in his council flat staring at a blank piece of cloth he had bought that day to make a banner for the Moorland's Estate Anti-Poll Tax Union. Finishing his can of lager he picked up a paintbrush and slowly began to write out the words as best he could. 'Moorlands' Estate Anti-Poll Tax UNION'. To add some design features he dashed some lines at odd angles between the words. Pleased with his efforts he sat on the couch and finished his beer as he waited for the paint to dry. The next day he would be carrying the banner into a tense stand-off against police outside Brixton Town Hall.

While in Scotland the year before there had been some protests outside town halls, a year later in England and Wales there were larger protests and a more radical mood in the air. The scale of non-payment in Scotland was widely known and bolstered the movement south of the border, with especially large crowds in the south of England. Towns that hadn't seen protests since the Corn Laws in the 1820s or the Chartist movement in the 1840s were now witness to large gatherings, with nervous councillors calling in police reinforcements in a number of towns from Kent to Cornwall.

Walton Town Hall in Surrey saw nearly 1,000 people gathered outside, throwing eggs and chanting as the Poll Tax rate was set at £448 per person.[25] In Brighton protestors got into the council chamber ahead of the budget meeting and occupied the councillors' seats, conducting a ridiculous parody of a council meeting and stamping on hundreds of coloured balloons before being ejected by security. A Tory councillor fumed, 'It was a disgraceful show of so called "people power"!'[26] The subsequent meeting was deadlocked when seven Labour councillors broke ranks and voted with the Tories to reduce the level of the tax by £30 to £342.50. By 3.45 a.m. a decision had still not been made, so the exhausted councillors trooped home, frustrated and dispirited.

There was a protest in Bath attended by 750 people, at which eggs, flour and stink bombs were thrown at council officers. Some of these actions were not condoned by organisers, however. The Bath Trades Council organiser Stewart West gave the official line: 'it is a shame that there was a small group of people determined to disrupt things but most people were there to peacefully register their disgust at the Poll Tax'.[27]

Around 10,000 marched through Hastings, led by bagpipe and a huge banner saying 'don't let the rich get richer and the poor get poorer'. When they got to the rally in Wellington Square people hung a cardboard cut-out of Thatcher from a nearby tree to cheers. At the budget meeting on 8 March 1990 people threw flowers, coins and beer cans at the police guarding the town hall. Just along the south coast in Worthing 250 people held a rally organised by Jenny Pettit, a local housewife. The local newspaper the *Worthing Herald* made a big deal out of the copy of *Militant* held by Martin Porritt as he addressed the demo.[28]

In Norwich protestors shouted down the councillors in the chamber, unfurling a banner imploring them not to be 'Thatcher's lackeys'. Others stormed the town hall, breaking up the meeting by occupying the chamber and chanting and shouting, before heading to the basement, barricading themselves in and destroying computers and print outs. The council meeting had to be rescheduled for the following Sunday with even more police reinforcements drafted in to guarantee the councillors' safety.

One far-fetched police report of a protest in Plymouth claimed that of the 400 people present 50 were SWP, and alleged that they held up placards saying 'Kill the Police'. Further south-west, in Truro, 'A woman on horseback thrust a makeshift spear through a 20ft effigy of Mrs Thatcher outside Truro Cathedral Cornwall. The effigy was set alight and demonstrators surrounded police as a man was arrested'.[29] The demonstrators were clearly nothing if not inventive.

Nottingham Town Hall also saw a very creative direct action with protestors dressed as Robin Hood occupying the council chambers, chanting, singing and acting like merry men and women. The press reported seeing 'a man dressed as Maid Marian, who urged the council to resign'.[30] Things became heated however when someone threw shaving-foam 'pies' at some councillors. This led to security intervening and the police being called. Arrests were made. In Southampton 100 people got into the council's public gallery and started shouting, before one man lowered himself down into the chamber and started knocking the councillors' papers and documents off the tables. Outside, another 400 protestors tried to ram the doors to get inside before they were set upon by police with truncheons and riot shields, resulting in 27 arrests. The police report noted that several people from 'the Student Union' and NALGO were also present.

A march in Colchester started off peacefully enough until it made its way past the Conservative Club, where it was greeted by jeers and insults from the Tories inside. Some items were thrown at the windows and the police moved in to make arrests, leading to the inevitable altercations. To deflect blame, one Inspector Tanner reported in the press the following day that the violence was the result of a conspiracy, allegedly agreed four days in advance by a small group of Trotskyists and anarchist collaborators.[31]

In London the protests were bigger and even angrier. At the Hackney Council Poll Tax setting session on 5 March, 500 people disrupted the meeting to the point where it had to be abandoned. The reconvened meeting a few days later was met by 5,000 people gathered in an angry demonstration – the level was due to be set at £499 per head. The charge still came with massive cuts, especially to the voluntary sector, which relied on council grants to survive. The police line in front of the town hall was met with a barrage of flour, eggs, bottles, sticks and beer cans, while a road sign pulled out of the pavement was used as a makeshift battering ram. Riot police attacked the protesters with batons and some responded by throwing bricks. Windows of local businesses were smashed and litter bins set on fire.[32] The subsequent police report admitted that 'although disorder was anticipated the numbers of demonstrators attending far exceeded intelligence forecasts'.

At the rate-setting meeting in Haringey there were chaotic scenes as hundreds stormed the civic centre in Wood Green to prevent councillors voting for a rate of £573. Six police were injured and 11 people arrested. Around 5,000 people demonstrated in Lambeth and there was also a fierce clash with the police as the crowd marched through Brixton and approached the notorious police station.

One researcher later estimated that, in all, there were 55 protests at council meetings across Britain, involving at least 22,000 people (using the newspaper figures, which can be conservative in their estimation).[33] The clashes in England were in stark contrast to the year before in Scotland, when the protests outside town halls had been angry but attracted little to no police intervention. Sheridan believed this was due to the police in England and Wales not respecting the right to protest: 'they waded in truncheons flexed. Confrontations between the cops and demonstrators took over the real business of embarrassing councillors.'[34] The scenes were filmed by local TV and the broadcast nationally. The sight of 'the sans culottes storming the civic centre', as Maureen Reynolds described it, showed that a real problem was brewing for the government.

Nevertheless Militant still got the blame. After the clashes outside the council chambers, Kinnock warned that people were 'being exploited by Toy Town revolutionaries who pretend that the tax can be stopped and the government toppled simply by non-payment'.[35] By this stage the official Labour position had hardened, and anyone advocating non-payment was a dangerous subversive playing politics with people's lives.

The spectre of Militant permeating and coordinating local protests was quite vividly portrayed in the press. Stroud was described as 'a hotbed of Militant activity', which struck most people on the far left and in Stroud as very funny. *The Sun* accused Militant of being 'Labour's own Inter-City Firm'. Bashing Militant was part of the media and right-wing agenda at the time because it fitted with the strategic objective of pressuring the Labour Party to expel the hard left. Many of the Poll Tax protesters were not Militant members and indeed Militant itself – believing that civic protest to put pressure on councillors was key – were usually less welcoming of militancy on demonstrations, criticising the anarchists for their apparent addiction to rioting and disruption. In Lothian, the Direct Action Movement proposed an occupation of the town hall, but the local Militant organisers described the action to the press as the work of 'a minority' who 'disrupted our plan to put our case in an orderly fashion to the council'.[36] For their part, anarchists criticised Militant for being essentially reformists who were using the Anti-Poll Tax movement to rejuvenate the class collaboration of Labour.

In the media the Tories' strategy was to excoriate Labour by blaming them for failing to keep their far-left 'hooligans' under control. After the protests outside Nottingham Council, Thatcher spoke in Parliament to 'utterly condemn the violent scenes organised by Militant Tendency. Like Grunswick and Wapping, it seems to be an abrogation of democracy'.[37] Commenting on the scenes in Hackney, she claimed the protest was 'organised, I understand from the excellent article in *The Times*, by the militant left'.[38] This was a clear attempt to blame organised political forces for what was rapidly developing into a mass movement with its own logic and dynamics.

The local government minister, David Hunt, added to Thatcher's charge by demanding a public inquiry into connections between Militant and Labour, saying their opposition to the tax was marked by 'confusion, deception, irresponsibility and illegality'.[39] Attempting to deepen the division in Labour, Thatcher once again called on Kinnock to disown the 28 Labour MPs who had publicly pledged to not pay.

As the hands of Labour councillors were tied by the party leadership, many were limited to simply urging people to claim their full rebates as a way of alleviating the onerous financial burden of the tax. Their focus was on those who were too impoverished to pay, a moral question that was perfect for Labour politicians: it highlighted the iniquity of the tax while avoiding the political question of widespread resistance. It also allowed the Labour leaders to cast themselves in the paternalistic role of tribunes of the poor – only they could protect the unfortunate wretches from Thatcherite excesses. In the meantime, everyone else should pay their taxes and wait for the election in 1992.

Within the Tory Party, however, there was growing concern about how things were playing out. At a meeting of the powerful backbench 1922 Committee, Conservative MP Tony Marlow warned that the government might be seen to be 'declaring war on the people'.[40] The balance of forces was still on the side of implementation, but the sheer scale of the opposition was exceeding even the most pessimistic Tory expectations.

Councils in crisis

A couple of years before the Poll Tax, the government had delivered a leaflet about the AIDs crisis to every house in the country. Now they planned to do it again with a leaflet titled *The Community Charge (The So-called 'Poll Tax'): How It Will Work for You*. But only a few days into the ambitious delivery schedule Greenwich Council lodged a legal challenge against the contents of the leaflet. A judge ordered an immediate halt to deliveries which caused frustrated rage in the Department of the Environment. Eventually the judge ruled against Greenwich council's challenge, but it was constant interferences like this which undermined the smooth operation of the machine.

Countering government messaging became key for oppositional councils. Lambeth – at the time led by Joan Twelves – carried an article on the front page of its free sheet *Lambeth People* titled 'Poll Tax – here are the facts!', which challenged each claim in the government's leaflet. Essentially the council predicted that claims the tax would be cheaper would be proved false, and argued that it was a huge data-gathering operation: 'some local observers predict that the Poll Tax will virtually mean a national identity scheme and computer records keeping track of the movements of every adult in the country'.

The argument that the tax was an invasion of privacy seems rather quaint given the digital age that followed and the huge amount of tracking that so many people voluntarily accept with smartphones and other technological breakthroughs – but in the late 1980s fears over personal data being stored in new networked computers were very real. Trafford APTU activists confronted their council about their registration forms which asked for details of people's personal relationships, a question which violated the Data Protection Act. The judges decided in their favour, forcing Trafford and other councils to scrap the registration forms.

Such was the chaos north of the border following stories spread by the refusenik campaign about extortionate Poll Tax bills that the government scrambled around for concessions to sweeten the bitter pill. Seeing the beginnings of a crisis in Scotland, Thatcher knew she had to act. Ridley was dumped as Secretary of State for the Environment after some inopportune comments to a journalist about greater integration with Europe (he had told the editor of *The Spectator* that if British sovereignty was sacrificed to German led-federalism then 'you might as well give it to Adolf Hitler, frankly'). He was replaced by Chris Patten. This move damaged the Prime Minister – Ridley was one of the last arch-Thatcherites in the Cabinet, a true loyalist. Thatcher had sacrificed him to save the tax but in doing so had left herself further isolated. As the crisis deepened this would leave her without an ally to rely on when the knives came out. Moreover, behind the scenes, Patten had been hostile to the tax. He was now handed the poisoned chalice and instructed to drink from it in front of the entire country – not a sound basis for ensuring a minister's reliability.

The practical issue of collection by the councils was raised repeatedly. An inner London authority might have had around 60,000 domestic rates to collect, but with a tax on individuals over 18 that would increase to over 200,000. In addition, the high volume of people moving between boroughs across the capital would make it very difficult to maintain accurate collection records. The rates had been easier to collect because they were based on properties, which, unlike people, did not move. Poll Tax registration had also proved to be a nightmare. The first real attempt to create a national database using computers was leading to all manner of errors concerning addresses and individuals. In Colchester registration forms were despatched to a public toilet. Of the 140,000 forms sent out in The Wirral, 50,000 were returned improperly filled in.

Alison Dixon, a GMB shop steward working at Manchester Council in the Poll Tax collections department, commented that 'it was chaotic. For a whole year the computer system was continually being switched off because the software was inadequate. If I got a telephone enquiry and hunted for the answer I would get six different replies because government legislation seemed to be changing each week.'[41] Most of the staff had been sent there from the dole offices, and only a small minority had actually applied to do the work. Diligence in the task at hand was almost non-existent, and morale was incredibly low. Dixon heard many people working on registrations say they wouldn't be registering themselves. Across the country it was clear that the computerised database was proving to be almost impossible to keep up to date. During the first year of the tax, Strathclyde Council officials were having to work at breakneck speed to update their records, with 40 per cent of the nearly 4 million entries having to be altered, averaging 10–15,000 changes a week.[42] This was compounded by the community campaign itself: around one in ten of the forms people could use to report on their neighbours came back with obviously bogus names. The work was long, frustrating and often fruitless.

A MORI poll in Lambeth published in March 1990 found that 84 per cent of people would be worse off under the new tax. As a result 35 per cent expected they would have to have cut back their spending on clothes and food. In a sign of how little resources people had, only 3 per cent believed they could fall back on their savings. By the time the tax had been in place in Scotland for a year and was about to be introduced in England and Wales, the financial implications were undeniable – lower income earners were losing out in the new financial arrangements. Households with incomes limited to £50–£200 a month lost the most, while richer people were paying far less than they had under the rates.[43]

The Citizens Advice Bureau in Manchester noted that when the bills started to come through hundreds of people showed up asking about the complicated rebates system. 'Two-thirds of our inquiries concerned rebates ... the profound distress and anxiety suffered by people on benefits and low incomes who received a full bill must not be underestimated.'[44] In other places the chaos of the computer system led to serious errors. There were several cases of children being summoned to court for non-payment. A woman in Hulme received a bill for her recently deceased husband for £6; 'it felt like an insult' she told local welfare campaigners.

Labour brooks no opposition

As D-Day drew closer in England and Wales, Labour turned up the heat on its rebels. The pockets of recalcitrant Labour councillors who had burned their registration forms and were publicly defying both the government and their own party were given short shrift. The NEC threatened to discipline Tower Hamlets councillors over their Anti-Poll Tax stand. They were forced to remove their pledge not to prosecute Poll Tax refusers from their local election manifesto. The local party explained their position: 'The reality is, people here are not going to be able to cope with the Poll Tax whatever we do. Labour councils, particularly in London, are going to be asking whether they must hound the most vulnerable people.'[45]

The NEC suspended 15 Liverpool councillors for the same reason, leaving them unable to attend even their own ward meetings. Their protest that they had only been carrying out the policy of the District Party fell on deaf ears.

Opposition from Labour politicians extended beyond just the council chambers. The sheer size of the mass movement in Scotland and the depth of its reach into working-class communities had stiffened the resolve of some of the local Labour MPs. Kinnock had a real headache dealing with outbursts from a number of them – mostly those in the left-wing Socialist Campaign Group (SCG) – which he rapidly repudiated at any opportunity. Glasgow Provan's MP, James Wray, publicly criticised his colleagues in the 'supposedly socialist' Strathclyde Council: 'They should not be adopting warrant sales for working-class people, especially the most vulnerable people in society, with the worst health conditions, the worst housing conditions, and the worst unemployment.'

Wray was from a poor Roman Catholic family raised in the Gorbals, and did not agree with the view that the Community Charge should be implemented merely because it was the law: 'If it's morally right to implement a good law it's morally right to break a bad one.'[46]

Another SCG member, Harry Barnes (MP for North East Derbyshire), shocked the Tories in the Commons by calling for mass civil disobedience to break the tax, saying 'I will break the law and gladly suffer the consequences as a legitimate means of protesting against an unjust measure.' This brought an angry riposte from the Minister of State, John Patten, who branded Barnes not the 'looney left but the lawless left!'[47] Barnes, however, also got into an argument with Militant over their campaign of mass non-payment; he was concerned that millions of people were potentially being led into a situation where they faced courts and prison for their defiance, without being fully aware of the dangers. Militant replied that while Barnes 'criticised the lack of fight from the Labour leaders ... unfortunately he has no real strategy himself'.[48]

Labour was thrashing around for a way to be relevant to the growing movement while also forcing its elected representatives to implement the tax to the full extent of the law. Running to catch up with the APTUs they proposed a national demonstration on 1 April – the day the tax was to be launched in England and Wales. Half-hearted efforts to persuade people to attend their protest rather than the demo on 31 March were met with understandable disinterest. In the end, they cancelled the protest for 'lack of money'. Instead, Bryan Gould, not famous for his strategic vision, wrote an article in *Tribune* calling on people to join the Labour Party to show their opposition.[49] The Labour line was clear: only an election and a change of government could scrap the Poll Tax. Kinnock continued to warn against 'futile illegality'.[50] The socialist firebrand turned moderate David Blunkett was regularly wheeled out to impress upon the rank and file the new perspective that 'we will be successful in removing the Poll Tax [only] by removing the Government which imposed it'.[51]

Meanwhile, members on the ground in Sheffield faced a struggle against their own council. After the District Labour Party and the Labour councillors voted to implement the tax, rank-and-file members fought to overturn the decision. This battle within the party between the membership and the elected representatives further isolated the councillors, who were being opposed by residents and their own members. For most of them, however, this merely hardened their hearts against the opposition.

People were already widely sceptical of Labour's willingness to mount any serious opposition to the Poll Tax. Not for the first time in its history, Labour's abstention from a mass working-class revolt created the space for more radical voices to emerge. As *Scotland on Sunday* described it: 'The mass non-payment campaign is being led by supporters of the Militant tendency largely because of the political vacuum left by the party leadership. The substantial support to the calls for non-payment is known to be more than an irritant to Labour's leaders.'[52]

Feeling that the initiative was slipping away from them, the right of the local parties were unsparing in their criticism. The Isle of Wight Labour Party, led by Robert Jones, decried the islands APTU as a 'dangerous and deceitful front for the Militant Tendency, and their most wicked attempt yet to mislead the general public'.[53] Labour denounced a leaflet produced by the APTU arguing that mass non-payment could become an 'unstoppable force to defeat the Poll Tax and bring down the Tory government', dismissing it as 'pure fantasy: political adventurism gone mad.' Jones's view, shared by many, was that Militant were playing politics with people's lives, and that when residents' goods were being auctioned to pay off their debts, the Militant Tendency, 'which uses people with a breath taking cruelty and cynicism in order to gain support for their crazed ideas', was just as much to blame as the Tories. For their part, the movement scorned Kinnock's methods. Referring to his conference speech in 1985 in which he rounded on Militant and Liverpool City Council, the Northern Region of the ABAPTF published a leaflet criticising the 'grotesque chaos of a Labour council summonsing people who can least afford to pay the Poll tax'.

For Militant the contradictions of leading a mass movement while also being in the Labour Party under sustained attack were beginning to take their toll. They were in the counter-intuitive position of arguing for people to join a party whose very leadership were condemning them. In their pamphlet 'How to Fight the Poll Tax', Militant restated their traditional view that 'the most effective way that ordinary people can voice their opposition to the cowardly and subservient policies of the Labour leadership is not by turning their back on the Labour movement, or by standing on the sidelines, but by actually joining the Labour Party and participating in the struggle to transform the Party into a fighting socialist organisation which defends the interests of ordinary working class people with the same iron determination with which Thatcher represents the rich and powerful.'

But the Labour leadership answered their appeal for unity defin-itively. In 1988, 'witch-finder general' (as she described herself in her autobiography) Joyce Gould, from the Labour NEC, visited Glasgow to speak to local organisers about identifying and removing known Militant activists. Sheridan was already on their radar but his work in the Poll Tax movement had put a spotlight on him as a primary target for expulsion. In July 1989, around 20 members in Pollok were banned from holding positions in the party and an entire ward was suspended. Sheridan was expelled from Labour in October 1989. He was phlegmatic about his expulsion; he knew it was coming, and the trial – as with most left members in those days – was a fait accompli. In many ways it freed him up to be more radical and forthright without having to look over his shoulder at a possible disciplinary. It also got several Militant members thinking that perhaps their long-term Labour Party entryism strategy – which they had been pursuing since the 1950s – was coming to an end.

6

The Battle of Trafalgar (Square)

The next step was to bring all the various campaigns together in a huge public show of strength. The STUC had passed a motion calling for a national demonstration in the spring of 1990 to coincide with the launch of the tax in England and Wales and the year anniversary of its implementation in Scotland. On 24 September 1989, the Fed steering committee agreed a motion to welcome the call made by Campbell Christie and the STUC for a nationwide demo on 1 April backed by the TUC and Labour. However, the motion also noted that 'in the event that the British TUC refuses to organise such a national demonstration then this conference recognises that the All Britain Federation would have to take the task on board'.

They were right to be cautious. Efforts to get coordinated action, even a demonstration (let alone strike action), from the TUC were proving to be a labour of Sisyphus. But even troubled Sisyphus had an easy job compared to the left's battle in Labour itself. Dave Nellist led the charge to win Labour's NEC over to backing a demonstration – there was a close vote of 13 for and 14 against. Some of the softer left like Blunkett had been willing to back a protest, since it might at least give the impression that Labour was taking a more active approach. But Roy Hattersley rallied the right and argued the proposal down.[1] After that point the Labour leadership was not just unmoveable, they were outright hostile.

Labour having pulled the plug on the 1 April demo, it was clear the movement had to rely on its own resources. The Fed announced 31 March – a Saturday, and the day before the tax was launched – as the new date. Activists referred to the 31 March protest simply as 'The Demo' – an indication of the kind of focal point it became. Tony Benn and others made the case for a big, united protest against the tax, which was proving to be such a lightning rod for discontent against Thatcher in general. Benn had grown increasingly frustrated with Labour's hostility to the campaign, recording in his diary: 'The Labour Party is more frightened of the Anti-Poll Tax campaign than of the Poll Tax itself.'[2]

In the two months before the protest the movement organised around 6,000 actions, including demonstrations, public meetings and lobbying councils.[3] The mood of defiance was growing. Harold Lewis, a 69-year-old councillor from Blackpool, stated at a meeting of the local trades council that he would rather spend his retirement years in prison than pay the tax. In Manchester on 3 March, 5,000 people gathered to protest the tax. A sound system blared out Tracy Chapman's 'Talkin' bout a Revolution', while uniformed ambulance workers fresh from their strike marched alongside students and the elderly. Trade Union banners were on full display. From the stage, NUS executive member Andrea Enisouh inspired the crowd: 'We want the real democracy that the workers are fighting for in Russia, for control over what we produce. We want genuine socialism.'

Crucially for what was to come, it was not just traditional urban Labour areas where there were protests. Around 10,000 people demonstrated in Tunbridge Wells, as did 8,000 in Plymouth and 5,000 in Taunton. This was making some Tories in relatively safe seats begin to fret. Carl Learmand of the Granby Abercromby APTU summed up the mood of defiance: 'If they want it come and get it. We have more than an army waiting for them.'

By then it was clear that The Demo would be large. Reports were coming in of coaches across the country being booked. But on the steering committee of the ABAPTF there was some debate over the scale of the demonstration. Burns believed that Militant had seriously underestimated the size of the protest – they reckoned it might only be 20,000 strong. Militant wanted protests but saw them as only an auxiliary to the main struggle which was non-payment. Some believed that Militant's fixation on the non-payment campaign was in danger of making their vision and range of tactics too narrow. Months prior to the demonstration, Nally and Wally Kennedy, who was due to be the chief steward on the day, met with the Metropolitan Police, telling them to expect around 30,000 people. The police chief laughed – their intelligence suggested far fewer numbers. But by Christmas 1989 it was clear to organisers The Demo would be massive. Over a million leaflets were printed advertising it.

When the protesters gathered in Kennington Park in north Lambeth, ahead of marching to a rally in Whitehall it became clear just how big the protest would be. Kennington Park was the site of the great Chartist protest of 1848, a day when there had been rumours of an armed march on Parliament, a possible revolution and the overthrow of a government. That threat had been ended by surrounding the protest with tens of thousands of soldiers and special constables recruited specifically for the job of putting down an insurrection.

In 1990, there was a sense of history for many gathered in that south London park. Kennington was soon full of people from across England and Wales. Nearly 1,000 coaches travelled to London from over 600 towns and cities. Two trains were chartered from Cornwall. There were loads of placards, some mass-produced by one of the Trotskyist groups, others home-made; some anarchist flags; a marching band. One participant described the feeling: 'the atmosphere was wonderful: like a carnival. People were happy, but this was not an empty, superficial happiness. This was a happiness based on strength and power. And it was happiness that grew and developed as people realised the sheer size of the demonstration and thus of the whole movement against the Poll Tax.'⁴ As the crowd passed a building site, two of the workmen started singing the Red Flag.⁵ Some protestors carried Union Jacks with the centre cut out, in solidarity with the Romanian revolution which had as its symbol the Romanian flag with the emblem of the Socialist Republic removed. Two people carried a massive bed sheet tied between sticks, emblazoned with a simple response to the Community Charge: 'Up Your Bum'. The police report described the march as it approached the river as 'reasonably good natured'.

Crossing the Thames and entering Westminster the protest swelled to over 200,000. As the demonstration made its way past Downing Street, angry shouts inevitably emanated from the crowd, along with a few cans and other rubbish hurled at the Prime Minister's central London residence. The wrought-iron gates at the entrance to the street had only just been installed due to fears of an IRA attack, and police stood nervously behind the bars. A large group of people began a sit-down protest, chanting 'Maggie, Maggie, Maggie, Out, Out, Out!' More police began to gather around the sit down, looking to clear the area. Some nervous stewards tried to move the sitting protestors along, hoping to get them to Trafalgar Square to complete the march, but they were ignored. One Militant steward berated the anarchists, 'You can't even change your socks, let alone society!'⁶ At 2.16 p.m. a police sergeant noted in his log: 'one arrest, bottles and missiles thrown ... prisoner removed from scene – punks concerned'.⁷

Then an almighty fight broke out in Trafalgar Square. The police started to strike protestors, leading to retaliation. Hundreds of baton-wielding police stormed out of the South African embassy in what appeared to be a prearranged move. They ploughed into the demonstration, sending people running in fear. From the Strand police mounted on horseback appeared, charging into the crowd. A woman failed to get out of the way in time and was knocked to the ground. The police thought they were in charge but hadn't bargained on the size of the protest or the anger of the protestors. People fought back and the sheer weight of their numbers forced the police to retreat. When a police car tried to drive through the crowd, a protestor lunged forward and smashed its windows before the driver accelerated to get away. At this point no one had control, neither the police nor the stewards. There was only the mass of people retaliating against the violence from the police.

As the police horses charged into the crowd, protestors started a chant of 'Stasi! Stasi!', comparing the British police to the hated East German secret police who were now being hounded by the democratic revolutionary movement on the other side of the Berlin Wall. The feeling that the protests in Britain were symbolically linked to the events in Eastern Europe was palpable among the crowd. The Poll Tax might have been a British issue but the sense of there being a simultaneous global movement was strong. An unguarded building site just off Trafalgar Square provided plenty of ammunition in the form of bricks, sticks and pieces of scaffolding for people to arm themselves with. The South African Embassy off the Square was set alight in solidarity with the anti-Apartheid struggle. This only added to the sense of chaos and danger as fire crews arrived and struggled to attend to the conflagration.

In the description given by one demonstration participant, Simon Crab: 'the noise and violence in the Square reaches an extreme pitch; screaming protesters, police helicopters, sirens, whistles, burning buildings, the medieval sight of horses hooves trampling an unconscious woman, a concrete block hitting a policeman's head, a metal bar through a van's window. The sky is full of missiles – bricks, bottles, wood – anything that comes to hand – raining down onto the police, their scared and bloodied faces visible through their visors.'[8]

One hundred and seventy feet above the demonstration, Admiral Nelson's statue stared dispassionately down as thousands of people fought with the police in front of the grand buildings of the faded British empire – the symbols and facades of a country that seemed to be dying. Edwin Landseer's bronze lion statutes nestled between the protestors who were chanting 'We are many, they are few!' and were themselves like lions rising from slumber.

Batons were striking at different parts of the protest, driving people in different directions. By this point, Tony Benn was demanding to speak to senior commanders. He went up to a line of police holding their ground, viewing them with suspicion, noting later in his diary that they might in fact have been soldiers in police uniform. The police chief blamed the violence on the protesters, but Benn did not believe him. 'I think that what they had done was break the march up, squeeze the people in the middle and frighten them, and then no doubt some bottles and things were thrown. It reminded me a bit of Wapping.'[9] Jeremy Corbyn had been due to speak, but the events of that afternoon meant that the final rally had to be cut short, much to the frustration of the demonstration organisers.

As the police struggled for control, protesters and tourists seemed to blur into one. Some people arrested at the end of the day had not been part of the protest at the beginning, they just saw the fighting and joined in, having their own grievances with the cops. Towards the evening, looting started around Charing Cross as music shops had their shutters torn off and guitars and keyboards were taken.

One story illustrates how the events in the Square were in no way reducible to the acts of isolated anarchists or violent opportunists. Zoe Young was a student at Sussex in 1990. She went up to London with her friends for the big demo. 'Amid all the mayhem one moment really stuck with me: somewhere near Trafalgar Square, riot going on all around us, an elderly lady was crying alone in the road. My boyfriend and I felt worried about her and I asked her if she needed any help. She said "don't you worry lass, I'm just so happy to see all these young and strong folk fighting to protect those of us that can't".'[10]

That evening a Class War spokesperson described the rioters as 'heroes', which led the shocked journalist to warn his viewers about the 'repugnant views being expressed'. Sheridan described them as 'idiots' who were detracting from the main message but were not an organised conspiracy. He and Nally were whisked away to TV news stations to explain themselves as representatives of the demonstration organisers. Concerned that the scenes played out around the West End would set the movement back, and under pressure from the news reporters to condemn the violence, Sheridan told the BBC, 'we condemn it totally … 200 to 250 of these individuals intent on causing trouble'. Nally and Sheridan both separately stated that the movement would hold an 'internal inquiry', 'root out the troublemakers' and 'name names'. Inevitably, these comments enraged many activists. Nally received death threats after the protest. Sheridan later justified his comments, saying he had been overcome with revulsion at 'what a few people purporting to be demonstrators were doing'.[11] He emphasised that he deplored the actions of the police and condemned their tactics, but it was his anger at the rioters which upset so many people. There was no internal inquiry after the demonstration, but the sense of being policed by their own side drove a real wedge between Militant and some of the other campaigners.

Essentially the falling out was over the attitude to rioting. Militant's fear was twofold. Firstly, they were worried about a potential backlash within the Labour Party if they were accused of perpetrating a riot. Secondly, while they condemned the actions of the police, several in Militant believed that the protest had been infiltrated by either under-cover police – agent provocateurs – or anarchists or both. They believed that rioting was not a genuine socialist, working-class act.

From the anarchists' perspective, the events in Trafalgar Square were a festival of the oppressed. The view of the more radical wings could be summed up by a phrase made popular on the punk rock scene by Kurt Cobain from Nirvana: 'Vandalism: As beautiful as a rock in a cop's face.' For anarchists there is something emancipatory about the violence of the oppressed – it has a liberatory impulse, a crowd of people finally freeing themselves from fear of the police and the state. As opposed to Kinnock's view that violence was alien to the British working class, anarchists pointed to a long tradition of organised resistance dating back hundreds of years: 'everything we have ever gained has been through fighting'.[12] *Living Marxism*, the journal of the Revolutionary Communist Party, was just as forthright: 'From *Militant* to *Marxism Today*, most of the old left has objected to the violence on the grounds that it will alienate traditional Tory voters and other moderates from the Anti-Poll Tax campaign ... these groups risk alienating the very people who are most important to the revolutionary project – working class youth. It we want to overthrow the exploitation and oppression of the old world and build a new society, we will find that those prepared to confront a baton swinging mounted policeman make far better allies than do disaffected Tory shopkeepers.'[13]

Other revolutionary socialist groups – while not fetishising the violence in the way some of the anarchists did – were sympathetic to the protestors and highly critical of the response by Militant. Several of the people involved in the fighting were socialists who had also been active in the miners' strike and in the Wapping resistance to Rupert Murdoch's attempt to break the print unions. They had seen police violence against picket lines, and witnessed first hand the new semi-militarised police with their new weaponry and tactics. They saw Militant as being soft on the police, with an aversion to radical action that led to compromise when it came to confronting the violence of the state.

Sheridan was unimpressed by the 'creative violence' of anarchism, contemptuously deriding the anarchists as a bunch of rebellious posh kids: 'Daddy was a stockbroker and mummy was a head teacher … a pampered and privileged rebellion.'[14] Anarchists hit back, accusing Militant of being police narks and sell outs, more interested in boosting Labour reformism than actually fighting the tax. There was a feeling that Militant were angry because the working class were rising up in 'the wrong way', a way that did not accord with their preconceived plans and perspectives.

It was not like rioting was an unknown thing in the Thatcher years. In both 1981 and 1985, rioting in inner city communities – often with large black populations – had led to much national soul-searching and debates in the press about urban decline and the re-emergence of mass structural unemployment which, due to racism, was inevitably more prevalent among young black people. These protests were easily dismissed as the actions of a violent underclass, or the result of misunderstandings between the police and the communities. But the protest on 31 March 1990 was the biggest riot that London had seen in over a hundred years, and it could not be explained away so easily. There had been physical confrontations between the police and unemployed protestors in 1932, when right-wingers enlisted as special constables beat the hunger marchers as they tried to get into Trafalgar Square.[15] The fact that the Poll Tax riot took place in central London too, not in one of the urban areas in Zones 2 and 3, and that tourists had been witness to clashes just five minutes' walk from the heart of government, did not sit well with the establishment. After the riot the police concluded that they had lost control due to poor strategy on the day. They had tried to clear out the Square to disperse the crowd, but this only resulted in groups of people targeting other places across the West End. It also meant that the protestors mingled with other Londoners and tourists, making them harder to identify and adding to the numbers. Some people arrested for rioting and affray on the day had not been on the demonstration but just got caught up in it.

In Glasgow, however, a sizeable Anti-Poll Tax march on the same day went off relatively peacefully, with only a handful of arrests for minor offences. The protest organisers were even praised by the Assistant Chief Constable of Strathclyde.[16] Malcolm Rifkind opined, 'I thought it was a pity the English could not be as law-abiding as the Scots.'[17]

Rumours that police provocateurs had started the trouble circulated in various quarters. There was at least one undercover policeman on the demonstration. John Dines was an officer in the Special Demonstration Squad, posing as an activist using the name John Barker. He had infiltrated anarchist networks, even starting a relationship with Helen Steel, who later become one of the defendants in the McLibel trial. Dines even contributed an article to the AK Press pamphlet on the riot, describing 'a charge by about 20 cops, truncheons out, fists, boots flying into kids, women, the old, whoever got in their way – I was soon to meet the gutter.' His article reads like a pretty standard anarchist tract of the time, with a heavy dose of anti-police invective and a celebration of spontaneous working-class violence. Dines even designed a poster to raise funds for the arrested protesters – he used a photo of a woman about to strike a policeman, with the slogan 'disarm authority, arm your desires'.[18] How many police provocateurs there were at the protest might never be known, but they existed, and were an indication of how seriously the state took the movement.

Parliamentary fall out

The real crisis for the establishment was that the militants were becoming the leaders of a 'mob' that included, in Thatcher's words, 'law-abiding, decent people'. Those law-abiding, decent people were the bedrock of Conservatism – if they turned against the government over the tax then the party was finished at the next election. The sight of mass public disorder – beyond the control of any institution or individual, and not something that could be bargained or compromised with – was a terrifying spectacle for the powers that be. Alan Clarke MP took a different tack however, dismissing the protestors as 'all the anarchist scum, class-war, random drop outs and trouble seekers that had infiltrated the march'.[19]

Fresh from the protest, George Galloway warned in the Commons the following week: 'If the Government does not change course on the Poll Tax, it is going to be a long hot summer.' The Home Secretary David Waddington shot back that Galloway's words 'could be easily interpreted by people outside this House as an incitement to violence'. Waddington went on to inform the House of the casualties: '374 police officers injured, together with 86 members of the public and 20 police horses; 339 people arrested for public order and other criminal offences, including riot, affray and criminal damage; about 250 reports of damage to property.'[20]

Labour's attitude to the Poll Tax demonstrated the simple truth of its existence as an electoralist and constitutionalist party. Its function was to pass laws that would gradually improve people's lot in life, and therefore it also had to accept laws passed by the Tories, since the sovereignty of Parliament had to be respected. The contradiction for Labour's reformist leadership has always been that the workers' movement more generally is occasionally prone to anti-constitutionalist action, dating back to the Chartists in the first half of the nineteenth century.

The response to the Poll Tax rioting from the Labour establishment was one of horror. Goaded by Tories in Parliament that the Labour Party was overrun with radicals, Kinnock scornfully jibed back: 'When it comes to extremists, the difference between us is this: I *fight* them, the Prime Minister needs them.'[21] Labour right-winger Roy Hattersley joined the Tories in condemning the rioters 'without reservation or qualification', and supported calls for inquiries into the protest, adding 'it is inconceivable that violence on such a scale was spontaneous.'[22] The view from the barricades was quite different however. Iain, an APTU activist from a small town in Hertfordshire, remembered that the protest largely consisted of people 'chucking stuff and being angry, but it served a purpose, it began to convince people in power that the tax was a bad idea'.

The day after the protest, Benn found a message left on his answer machine: 'you fucking cunt. Now you've lost the next election for us.'[23] However, despite both the rioting and Labour's vocal official complaints about the grassroots movement, the party enjoyed a huge boost in the polls, putting them 24 points ahead of the government. Thatcher's personal approval rating slumped to 23 points, lower than it had been in 1981. This was the beginning of the end for the Iron Lady. The resistance was starting to win, and if Labour played its cards right then it could be the direct beneficiary.

7

A Ragtag Army

'The rich man in his castle, the poor man at his gate.
Says Thatcher, "I'll make you equal, you can both pay standard rate."'

Despite the ferocious explosion of rage on The Demo, it was not the riot that stopped the Poll Tax. It was the long, hard work of resisting the bailiffs and frustrating the courts. The summer of 1990 was an intense period of activity for the Poll Tax rebels, one where the status quo seemed to be crumbling more generally. It was not just in Bucharest, Berlin and Moscow that large protests were happening. On the evening of the Poll Tax demo in Trafalgar Square, prisoners in the decrepit Strangeways Prison staged a sit-down protest in the chapel against the violence of the prison guards and the dehumanising routine of strip searches and 23-hour lock ups. Their campaign lasted 25 days, including a rooftop occupation and protests against the atrocious cramped conditions they lived in. Some of the prisoners hung a banner from the roof with the slogan 'No Poll Tax Here' – an ironic sign of solidarity with the movement, because prisoners were exempt from the tax. It was probably one of the few things they did not have to complain about.

Back in Westminster, away from the overcrowded prisons and the impoverished inner city sprawls, there was serious disquiet among Tory MPs. Whispered plots in the Westminster bars and over dinner tables in the shires were becoming louder, and the 1922 Committee was beginning to get worried. Every aspect of the Poll Tax was going wrong. It was not raising more money, it was proving to be expensive to collect, a riot had just broken out in central London, and Thatcher seemed to be responding to the crisis by doubling down. This was the flagship policy after all. Tory MPs began to wonder if the flagship was holed below the waterline, and if so, whether should the captain go down with her ship.

Despite the opposition the councils obeyed the law. Medina Council on the Isle of Wight was the first in England to take residents to court for non-payment. The local APTUs put a call out for everyone who was summonsed to attend the court and plead their case. Steve Nally travelled there on behalf of the Fed to see the court-case process first hand. Hundreds of people arrived at the court to see the judge. Some were so poor they had walked across the island because they could not afford the bus. Nally noted how local people seemed meek at first, over-awed by the legal pomp and circumstance, but after a few judgements 'they began contesting the court and its arrogant officials'. Each case was taking over an hour to be heard, as Alan Murdie and other lawyers who supported the campaign challenged each dot and comma of the bills and summonses and pleaded on behalf of the defendants. The delay tactics and disruption caused the judge to throw out 3,800 cases. The mood among campaigners was jubilant.

The events on the Isle of Wight convinced the Fed that the courts would be crucial in the battle to defeat the tax. Following similar actions by Poll Tax refusers, South Tyneside and Wandsworth dropped cases against a large numbers of non-payers. By this time the movement had developed its rhythm. In Scotland the focus was on blocking the sheriffs, in England and Wales it was on the courts. It was now a war of attrition, a question of which side could wear the other down first.

Between 1990 and 1991 there were 4.7 million summonses and 3.3 million liability orders issued in England and Wales. In the summer of 1990, Strathclyde Regional Council released their official payment figures: 520,000 people were not paying the tax. In Scotland refuseniks were already making their way through the courts; England and Wales were only beginning to follow by July. Councils were looking to issue summonses to obtain liability orders, allowing them to send in the bailiffs. For some APTUs this meant a shift of the battleground from agitation on estates and in communities to the practical work of legal defence in the courtrooms. The problem for the councils was the sheer volume of non-payers. This was an indication that the non-payment campaign was having an impact. To speed things up, the councils had initially hoped to push through 500 non-payers at a time in a rubber-stamping exercise. Council officials believed that most people would not turn up to court, allowing them to quickly get the liability orders simply by reading out their names to the magistrates. This would allow the council to claw back missing tax money from wages or income support – though it was more likely that they would simply send in the bailiffs.

The movement had to ensure that people were not railroaded through the system and were supported. Each person summonsed had the right to an individual hearing if they chose it, and the movement encouraged them to do so. The vast majority of people up before the judges had never been near a court before, and the entire legal system was designed to be intimidating and overwhelming. Most APTUs provided 'McKenzie friends' for the defendants. The right to be accompanied in court had been established after the *McKenzie vs McKenzie* divorce case in 1970, allowing a companion to 'attend a trial as a friend, to take notes and quietly make suggestions and give advice'. The McKenzie friends had no right of audience – they could not address the court themselves – but they could provide invaluable moral support and some legal knowledge to people who might be utterly baffled by some of the terminology and intimidated by the austere nature of the court.

Appearing before the magistrates was often quite upsetting for defendants: 'People were generally horrified by the way in which the magistrates refused to listen to their arguments; talked over them; and generally attempted to herd them through like sheep. Commonly they would come out swearing at the magistrates and shouting that this was a kangaroo court.'[1] One Nottingham activist, Carolyne, wrote: 'my first appearance was on 13 December and any apprehensions I had soon disappeared on witnessing the mass congregations of people in the court foyer. There were at least two hundred of us, people from all walks of life coming together to voice protest against such an abhorrent tax.' In Hove, Mr Dewey, a maintenance worker, pleaded with the bench: 'We've got two children and I'm the only one working. They want £600 Poll Tax which is double what I used to pay in rates.'[2]

Some campaigners publicly flouted attempts by the courts to punish them. Martin Carlin, the secretary of Newham APTU, was at the head of a march to the court where he was due for a hearing, but fled the scene minutes before it started. This led to a police hunt after he went into hiding. It was later announced that he would be speaking at a public meeting while still a fugitive. 'If they want me so bad they know where I'll be', he told a local reporter.[3] Carlin also infuriated local Labour councillors by urging people to call them day and night to lobby them over the tax and the jailings.

One central aspect of the non-payment campaign was providing free legal advice to people going through the courts. The goal was to both keep people out of prison but also to frustrate the legal machinery for as long as possible to make the tax uncollectable. In Dover Court the chairman of the bench had 30 protesters ejected for rowdiness. Beyond the usual heckling and disruption, campaigners were outraged when the council presented written evidence against people but refused to let them see it. Bill North, acting as a McKenzie friend, was removed after he broke courtroom etiquette by shouting at the bench that 'people here are being treated worse than criminals. They should be able to see the evidence against them. It is a travesty of justice, a farce!'[4] Maria Walsh pleaded that she had no money and was pregnant, only to be met with the retort 'that is nothing to do with this court.' Aghast, she responded, 'I am gobsmacked, why are we here?'

The war of attrition in the months following the Trafalgar Square riot began to have an impact on the justices who were supposed to be over-seeing civil cases. Ian Lomax, Clerk to the East Hertfordshire Justices, decried 'the current state of magistrates services in some parts of the country, i.e. cancelled courts, staff shortages, etc., may lead a cynic to suggest that the next few months ought to be viewed with the optimism of the Titanic embarking upon its maiden voyage'.[5] In Hampshire, June Hanam, a magistrate of 22 years experience, quit over the tax: 'For the first time since we hanged people for sheep stealing we have got an unjust law on the statute books.'[6] Edward James from Aylesbury also resigned as a magistrate, declaring the tax to be 'so uncaring and uncompassionate as to be disloyal'.[7] In early 1991, 2,000 non-payers turned up at Camber-well Court, singing and chanting in defiance of both the police and the fire chief who arrived and told them to leave as they were causing a fire hazard. By 11 a.m. there was an adjournment because the prosecutor had vanished – he literally ran away. Just after lunch the court officials arrived and announced that there would be no business in the court that day.[8]

The Labour left

The 'fighting 50' Scottish MPs who had publicly declared they would not pay the Poll Tax had been reduced to only 12 by January 1990. Those still holding out were a handful of Labour MPs who were prepared to break the law. Dennis Canavan, the MP for Falkirk West, was faced with a £50 fine for refusing to even register. He mischievously addressed an APTU meeting saying: 'This kind of public meeting is one kind of extra-parliamentary activity, and I am not telling people what to do, but if we get a mass civil disobedience or millions not paying the Poll Tax, that is the only way we can defeat it ... British people do not like unfairness, and this is the most unfair tax ever introduced.'⁹ As the tax was rolled out across England and Wales other politicians stood up against it. Brent East MP Ken Livingstone was summoned to court, as was MEP Mike Hindley and Jeremy Corbyn MP for Islington North. Corbyn appeared at Highbury Magistrates for not paying his Poll Tax bill of £481, declaring to *The Times*: 'I am here today because thousands of people who elected me just cannot afford to pay.' He was joined by 16 other constituents who were charged with non-payment.

The most famous MP tax-refusenik was Terry Fields. Fields was a member of Militant and as MP had only accepted a salary of £28,000 – the average for a skilled worker. For non-payment of £373 he was sent to prison for 60 days, longer than average and clearly intended to make an example out of him. He was the first public figure to be imprisoned, garnering him significant coverage in the newspapers. Labour's leadership immediately threw him to the wolves: 'Neil Kinnock has made clear that the Labour Party does not and never will support breaking the law'; Terry Fields was 'on his own'.¹⁰ Fields later bitterly told Tommy Sheridan: 'You'll find more humanity in prison than you will in the House of Commons.'¹¹

The antics of the Labour MPs refusing to pay inevitably brought the ire of Kinnock, who told the NEC that he had nothing but 'contempt for the irresponsibility of those who do not pay the Poll Tax when they can afford to pay'.¹² Chris Patten wrote a gloating letter to Kinnock, goading him on to drive the left out of his party: 'I was delighted to read in the newspapers this morning that you are attempting to rid your party of the extremist elements that have done so much to threaten the fabric of society, encourage law-breaking and wreak havoc in local government.'¹³ To help Kinnock's deliberations, Patten sent him a list of left-wing Labour MPs to expel, nearly all of them members of the SCG in Parliament.

In the Somerset town of Bridgwater, there was a by-election for a seat on Sedgemoor District Council in July 1990. Brian Smedley, the candidate of the Labour left, narrowly won selection by one vote against a Labour right-winger and fought an energetic campaign, mainly on an Anti-Poll Tax ticket. As he remarked: 'I was the only candidate of course who mentioned the 1381 Peasants' Revolt and impaling Poll Tax collectors heads on the town bridge.' Labour won the seat convincingly, and within a month the council chamber was occupied by protesters, who hung a massive banner up calling on councillors to break the law.

Smedley later wrote: 'The Tories were apoplectic with rage and indignation. Several stormed out, some responded aggressively to the protestors. Only the four Labour councillors remained in our seats.'[14]

Reforming the Community Charge

But the Tories had their own problems. In the first 18 months of the tax, 43 different proposals to alter it had been mooted by MPs, either sounding off to journalists or more formally raising the issue in the Commons. Two of them were major proposals designed to take the sting out of the huge bills. The first major adjustment had come in October 1989 with a proposal to provide an extra £1 billion for local government in England and Scotland to offset the tax. The regulations stipulated that no individual or couple should lose more than £3 a week moving to the Community Charge from the rates, so long as the local authority limited its spending to the government-advised levels. The £3 figure was based on a very optimistic formula of inflation at only 3.8 per cent and 100 per cent Poll Tax registration and payment. Given what the government already knew about Scotland that looked very unlikely. Then, with only months to go until 1 April 1990, a Special Transitional Relief policy was introduced whereby pensioners, disabled people or those in previously low-rateable homes who had not previously paid rates would get a deduction on their tax bill. This was designed to buy off the opposition, but it just made the councils' job even harder. The calculations they had to make for thousands of people eligible for rebates and relief measures were only compounded by the active sabotage efforts of local tax-refusers clogging up their mailboxes with endless correspondence.

All of this was exactly what Lawson had feared, expecting that the tax would end up costing the Treasury – the exact opposite of what was intended. From his new position on the backbenches he was freer to bask in the accuracy of his predictions.

Following this, CIPFA took the unusual step of briefing MPs about the Revenue Support Grant for that year, because 'the difference between spending assumptions ... and local authorities' existing spending plans is so wide and the implications of this for the Community Charge are so significant that the Institute considers that it needs to comment.'[15] This rattled a lot of Tory MPs, and there was more dissent growing. MPs worried about their seats, fretting over the daily headlines in the broadsheets. More of their constituents were being summoned to court, while photos of protests were splashed across the local papers. MPs like Corbyn were denouncing the Community Charge in Parliament as the most blatantly unfair form of taxation anywhere in the world.[16] The danger was not that left-wingers like Corbyn, Galloway and Nellist were saying such things – the Tories expected that – it was that now they were speaking for a mass movement.

More pressure was brought to bear on the government to act. In July 1990 it announced an extra £3.26 billion for local authority spending. This was largely supposed to offset the crisis of the original 'safety net' scheme whereby Poll Tax moneys had been redistributed from high resource (richer) to low resource (poorer) areas. This had seen several Tory councils hit their residents with massive Poll Tax bills to offset the high cost in places like Hackney, leaving many Tory voters to complain that the tax was penalising them – the opposite of what it was supposed to do. The safety net proposal was only supposed to last for four years before the 'unadulterated' Community Charge was implemented in each area, but already it looked like the financial reforms might not last that long.

Despite all the problems, Thatcher gave what *The Times* described as an 'assured performance' before the 1922 Committee, focused on maintaining strict austerity measures for public sector spending more generally. The extra money would come from different departments. This rearranging of the deckchairs on the sinking flagship meant Chris Patten received a warm reception from Tory MPs, who believed he had produced a generous package that would offset any possible electoral hit for the party while preserving the principles of the Community Charge.[17] The Transitional Relief scheme would be boosted to £570 million and only phased out over two years.

But the Poll Tax principles were already being broken. Its entire purpose had been to discipline local authorities under the guise of giving them more autonomy. But after several councils set spectacularly high charges the government had to cap their spending. This undermined the entire argument for the Tories' flagship policy.

The capping limit was essentially a continuation of the rate capping of 1985–86, which led 16 councils across the country to unite in opposition to try to defeat the government. The Department of Environment produced a formula for capping overspending councils that saw 20 local authorities – all Labour – have their budget reduced. The smallest reduction was in Hillingdon (where there was no overall control),

which had to shave £3.6 million from its budget to bring its Poll Tax
down by £53 per adult; the largest reduction was in Derbyshire, where
Patten imposed a £45 million cut on the council. The council leader,
David Bookbinder, grimly conceded that 'you cannot have cuts of this
magnitude without blood. This has been compelled upon us and it is
something we have always dreaded. There will be life after the cuts but
it will be pretty unpleasant.'[18] It was not just Labour councillors in Derbyshire; the Tories in Hillingdon were angry too. Tory leader Andrew
Boff was furious that the government had completely ignored a key philosophical reason for the tax – that it introduced accountability into local
government.[19]

Haringey introduced a £10 million cut but only reduced their Poll Tax
to £536, not the £508 the government had demanded. When queried
about this, the council admitted that their figures were based on a collection rate of 95 per cent, which they were nowhere near, therefore they
had to recoup the extra cost somehow. Patten intervened and denied the
council permission to send out revised bills. It seemed that whatever
reforms the government made they just caused more problems further
down the line. And these came from councils that were obediently
implementing the tax, setting aside the problems caused by the mass
non-payment movement.

Trade union paralysis

Despite the emerging national crisis, most trade unions remained rigidly
inactive, stuck to the spot. Their leaderships were totally wedded to
Kinnock's approach to the tax – denounce it but stay away from anything
that might stop it. A handful of unions had voted to endorse non-payment,
including the National Union of Journalists, BECTU (Broadcasting,
Entertainment, Communications and Theatre Union) and the National
Communication Union. When it came to non-collection, however,
union activists had limited success convincing the rank and file to take
any action.

There was some radicalism from individual union branches. In
Sheffield, 36 housing workers walked out on 6 April 1990, refusing to
attend Poll Tax training that fell outside their current job description and
union agreements. Four days later the entire housing department walked
out when managers who were not relaying information on the training
events were threatened with disciplinaries. The council responded by

sending letters to each worker urging them to return to work, offering individual deals and bypassing the negotiation procedures agreed with NALGO. In general, workers still limited their concerns to terms and conditions – issues like the regrading of staff for extra responsibilities, dealing with heavier workloads, and accommodation in cramped council offices. In Barnsley a school sacked four music teachers due to cuts from the capping which led to a strike by their teaching comrades.

Greenwich NALGO housing workers walked out after some of them were sacked for refusing to collect the Poll Tax without the necessary pay changes; their colleagues organised an indefinite strike demanding reinstatement. Lothian NALGO voted to support the protests against warrant sales. Glasgow CPSA members staged a 24-hour strike in the DSS Office against benefit deductions (withholding welfare to pay Poll Tax debts). A number of DSS workers boycotted filling out the NHB10(CC)s forms which provided details of claimants so their benefits could be cut. Disciplinary action in some London offices led to walk outs by members of the CPSA union in defence of their colleagues.

In June 1990 there was one last concerted push to try and engage the unions. A conference was called of trade unionists opposed to the tax to explore ways of taking industrial action. Assembled in Liverpool Central Hall, the turnout was impressive – 1,281 delegates representing over 870,000 union members from 651 trade union bodies. While the speeches were combative and the mood was positive, the delegates were mostly the usual suspects and the conference failed to break the logjam in the union movement towards taking concerted action.

'Stand firm we are winning'

Guildford Magistrates court, November 1990: 'Based on your experiments how dangerous would the pie have been?' asked the lawyer. 'Well, by throwing the pie at the frame it was possible to determine the terminal velocity of the pie at contact and its kinetic energy', replied the forensic scientist.

The discussion of the consistency and relative danger of a shaving-foam pie took place at the trial of four protestors who were up on charges related to common assault and obstruction after a protest at Nottingham Council House saw Guy Waddington throw 'custard pies' in the face of Conservative deputy leader Ted Hickey, as well as councillors Alan Clark and Shaukat Khan. The pandemonium in the council chamber disrupted the meeting to the point that the mayor had to stop proceedings in a hail of toilet paper and shaving foam. Police reinforcements had eventually arrived and made the arrests, as well as chased a number of other people out.

Labour leader Betty Higgins scolded the protesters: 'I understand why people are so against the Poll Tax, but I don't think this is the right way to deal with it.' This view summed up the general Labour Party response to the tax – it was a shame and a national scandal but people shouldn't do anything practical to stop it. For its part, the *Nottingham Evening Post* editorial admitted that the protest had the air of a 'student prank', before concluding darkly 'but those pies could have been bricks' and calling for more security.[20]

The courts took a dim view of the 'pies', made of shaving foam on paper plates. Keith Duncombe and Guy Waddingham were each sentenced to one month in prison for assault. Two others were given conditional discharges for two years and fined £250 each. Duncombe had totally denied throwing the pie at councillor Barbara Ricks, and in fact another protester admitted to throwing it in her testimony in court but the judge refused to believe her.

The Nottingham Defence Fund remained defiant, recognising that the sentences were intended to teach the local APTU 'a lesson'. 'The lessons we can learn are not to underestimate the state's power to do what it likes and to realise we must be hitting them where it hurts if they are taking us so seriously. The councillors had argued that they were intimidated by the protestors, the protesters pointed out that the councillors were sending in sheriffs and bailiffs and potentially imprisoning people.'[21]

By the end of June 1990 – two months after the Trafalgar Square demonstration – it was calculated that around 20 per cent of people in England and Wales had not yet made a single payment. A survey in the *Independent on Sunday* found that in Greenwich and Tower Hamlets non-payment was at 50 per cent, and only 25 per cent had been collected in Hackney. Rotherham collected only 40 per cent of its total amount, Oldham 32 per cent, and Rochdale 30 per cent.[22] By the end of the year, local authorities outside of Scotland claimed to have collected an estimated 73 per cent of the tax.[23] But the *Guardian* produced figures to indicate that, by December 1990, only 28 per cent had been collected.[24] It was obvious there was either total confusion or a serious amount of spin as to how effective the tax collection was. One thing was clear – the scale of non-payment, especially in areas with very active campaigns, defied even the most pessimistic predictions of the government. By May 1991, 56,000 people in Nottingham, roughly a quarter of the city, hadn't paid a penny towards their tax bill. Taking into account those who had only paid some of their tax, half the city had paid less than half or nothing at all. In Islington, only £4 million out of the £20 million due had been collected. The BBC reported on 6 March 1991 that roughly 14 million people had either paid nothing or were behind with their tax payments.

The defiance remained solid. Witham Against the Poll Tax put a robust moral case for non-payment: 'Don't listen to the clap trap about "breaking the law". Principles and justice come before any bad class laws.' This revolutionary challenge to the legal system – arguing that the law was not neutral and was ultimately related to class and power – was not uncommon in APTU literature.

Crawley Council took 2,000 residents to court for non-payment and 235 had liability orders issued. On one day of mass summons 30 people protested, and Bill North, President of the Sussex APTU, was thrown out by court officials, shouting 'I refuse to pay the Poll Tax out of principle and I will go to prison if I have to.'[25]

In normal situations the state would be expected to win cases against those who refuse to pay their taxes. After all, the state has power and the law on its side, and all it has to do is cajole, threaten and imprison enough people to make it work. But this was not a normal situation, and the local state was struggling too – the sheer scale of the opposition was hard to manage. The campaign had succeeded in gumming up the works sufficiently that many Poll Tax departments were simply over-whelmed with residents requesting rebates, challenging minor typos in their letters, asking for an adjournment of court appearances and so on. The volume of correspondence became unmanageable.

The councils tried to clear the backlog by putting hundreds of people through the courts at the same time, expecting magistrates to hand out judgements in only a few minutes. This often led to the formation of new APTUs as people were summoned by area and would end up meeting and talking in the court waiting rooms. It also led to a variety of creative tactics to delay court proceedings for as long as possible. There was no legal aid for Poll Tax cases so amateur legal advice from campaigners was invaluable when it came to helping people through the process.

As soon as a local APTU found out about a court summons they would dispatch activists. By this time councils were trying to process up to 4,000 people a day. Most did not show up, which was a mistake because the judge would then just rubber stamp them for a liability order. Those that did turn up were accompanied by McKenzie friends and given briefing materials to prepare them. The McKenzie friends were so effective at providing support and advice that in January 1991 Lord Justice Watkins at the High Court intervened to declare that judges had complete discretion over allowing lay representatives into the court, effectively resulting in McKenzie friends being banned from most proceedings. This enabled the courts to speed through batches of confused and nervous non-payers much more quickly. The Watkins decision was later overturned by the Court of Appeal after a campaign by lawyers from the movement.

One leaflet handed out in the North West described the best filibuster tactics to use in court:

> Say your defence is that the council has not sent you a bill and a reminder, only a summons, then they have to prove that they did this, or say that they have not processed your rebate despite the fact that you have contacted them numerous times. Ask to see your name on the Poll Tax register. Ask to see a copy of the council resolution setting the Poll Tax level – take your time it is quite lengthy.
>
> Ask the courts to explain what a liability order means.
>
> Ask the court to explain the powers of a bailiff, can they force entry?

The leaflet ended with a message for all wavering tax resisters: STAND FIRM WE ARE WINNING.

The rougher end of the business

By this time there was too much at stake for the campaign to fail now. A protest was called for March 1991, the anniversary of the riot. Around 40–50,000 people gathered in London and marched to Hyde Park. The organisers were pleased with the turnout, but the lack of violent scenes meant it did not really make much of an impression on the national media.

In order to ease collection, councils approached newsagents and asked them to install payment points for the tax. They sold it to local people as a simple way of paying while buying the milk and a newspaper, and to the newsagents as a business opportunity because people would make purchases while they paid their Community Charge. When campaigners got hold of the lists of who was participating they pressured the newsagents to pull out of the scheme. Often this was done simply by going in and speaking to the owner, threatening to boycott the business if they helped the council. Some of the more intransigent newsagents ended up with a brick through their window to drive the point home.[26]

It was not just small shopkeepers who were targeted. The failure of the unions to organise any kind of collective resistance to the Poll Tax collection put a lot of their members in danger. Punk Aid's song 'Fuck the Poll Tax' had little sympathy for Poll Tax collectors or people reporting on their neighbours with lyrics like: 'Snooper on his own, caught in non-payment zone, steel capped Dr Martens crunch his bones.' Stuart Neate from Brighton NALGO warned that 'the Poll Tax is very unpopular and this is making collection difficult … we are aware our members could face abuse'.[27] Council workers sent out to post demands through letter boxes or to register residents were occasionally met with threats or even violence. One remembered being surrounded by a group of teenagers who threatened to hurt him; 'This is a no Poll Tax area!' one of them shouted. NUPE General Secretary Rodney Bickerstaffe promised action if his members were hurt: 'The people who collect this tax and check up on those who have not paid will face terrific hostility. There will be industrial action as staff face the backlash.'[28] The Arun Anti-Poll Tax Union press officer wrote to members asking them to be civil to the Poll Tax collectors: 'they are only doing their job. When going to the civic centre, or writing, be courteous.'[29]

Some people did not want to be courteous. The Poll Tax collection HQ of Cambridgeshire City Council was fire-bombed by persons unknown and Anti-Poll Tax slogans sprayed on walls nearby. NALGO urged the council to put more measures in place to protect their members on the front line.

Non-payers would organise against bailiffs and support each other during court summons. Bailiffs could be driven away through sheer force of numbers, though there were occasional clashes with them. Red Action, a recent split from the SWP, argued that bailiffs were 'no better than thieves or muggers and must be treated by activists and the community as such'. The London Fed compared bailiffs to vampires – they can only get into your home if you let them in. Bailiffs' offices were also targeted. Activists would either seek to gain entry by pretending to be trades people or postal workers or simply storm in and occupy. One bailiff remembered how their office 'ended up like something out of Beirut. It was wrecked. Every piece of furniture and equipment had to be replaced. They even vandalised the family photographs of one of the partners in the firm. They barricaded themselves in with filing cabinets and were in the office from early afternoon until two in the morning, when the police managed to get in.'[30] It did not stop at the offices – bailiffs homes were identified, their addresses published, and protests organised outside. In the Forest of Dean, bailiffs were set upon by locals who stripped them naked and tied them to trees before trashing their car. The bailiffs were reluctant afterwards to go back into such a tight-knit community after that humiliation.

Bailiffs would also try their luck, rinsing non-payers for money through fear and people's lack of knowledge of the law. When Kirklees council employed the bailiff firm Gaults to follow up 3,000 non-payers, Gaults sent out letters to everyone charging them £25 for issuing the letter, when in fact costs could only be incurred by a visit. The regional federation intervened and the council were forced to back down and rescind all the letters. In Scotland, however, sheriffs were increasingly forcing their way into the homes of vulnerable elderly people and single mothers.

The high level of activity was clearly exhausting for many campaigners. Some were attending meetings every evening, and then leafleting bus and train stations the next morning to hit commuters. Some bailiff-busting episodes ended up in physical confrontation, but others just involved long periods of waiting. And it was not just in the cities. When bailiffs threatened to visit the village of Bishops Lydeard near Taunton, half the village barricaded off every road in and out, stopping every car and demanding to know why there were driving through.[31] One campaigner remembered driving through Hertfordshire with a friend to sit with an elderly woman at her cottage for 10 hours because the bailiff had threatened to come round that day. The stay was perfectly pleasant with cups of tea and biscuits, but the nervous tension of waiting for the knock on the door was exhausting and draining.

The number of people being threatened with prison, and the continued psychological warfare against those who were too poor to pay the tax, inevitably led to retaliation. Local campaigns published the names, photos and addresses of local councillors who were backing the tax or supporting the use of bailiffs. Ostensibly this was done to make a democratic point – that they were elected representatives and should be held accountable for their votes, which were having such an impact on the poor. But the effect was also obviously intimidating, making councillors uncomfortable that their home address and photo were being plastered all over a town. This happened to both Tory and Labour representatives. In Lambeth some councillors went to the local press complaining that they had been woken at 5 a.m. by 'bailiff-busters' knocking on their door. A Labour councillor who had voted to send in the bailiffs claimed she had returned home to find the word 'scab' daubed in red paint across her door. Blame was apportioned thick and fast to people on the Labour left, though no one claimed responsibility.

The Hillingdon APTU published a poster headed 'WANTED FOR JAILING THE POOR' in thick black letters, with photos of Tory council leader Andrew Boff, the mayor Ken Abel and another councillor Douglas Mills. Boff was quoted in the local paper gloating that 'some people will be spending Christmas behind bars' for non-payment. Campaigners also published the office details and names and addresses of bailiffs they could identify. Many activists felt that since bailiffs were an instrument of intimidation and even possibly violence against people then they were fair game for being publicly exposed. Local newsletters rejoiced when they found out that some bailiffs had quit their jobs as a result of the stress.

By Christmas 1990, 85,000 people had appeared in court out of the 1 million summonsed, but only two had been sent to prison in England. They were a 21-year-old man from Grantham, Bryan Wright, who was jailed on 7 December 1990 and spent Christmas inside. He was followed by a Militant supporter, Patrick Westmore, chair of the local APTU, who was sent to prison for 14 days on the Isle of Wight despite pleading poverty. Newcastle was the first Labour council in England to apply for a commitment to jail 50 people in January 1991. After an outcry the council suspended the action for a month and instead invited the non-payers to individual meetings with the Poll Tax sub-committee to arrange payments. But when only four people attended they stepped up operations to get some people behind bars.

Importantly the movement kept the pressure up whenever someone was jailed. Seven hundred people protested outside the prison on Wright's first day inside, and a group visited the local Tory MP Douglas Hogg demanding that Wright be given full visitation rights. He was released after serving 14 days of his 21-day sentence. In fact a number of people imprisoned were released early by prison governors, who thought it was a waste of resources keeping them locked up.

The Anti-Poll Tax movement was also occasionally targeted by fascists from the National Front and the British National Party. In Exeter the local APTU group officers were mainly drawn from Anti-Fascist Activist cadre (AFA) who had been schooled in the hard knocks of fighting Somerset Nazis during the 1970s and '80s. One of the Exeter Anti-Poll Tax demos was attacked by a group of fascists who were driven off by large numbers of people. AFA and the APTU then printed up thousands of leaflets, pointing out that the far right were on the side of Thatcher. This seriously dented the popularity of the local fascist cause for some considerable time. When Sheridan and his comrades were camped out in George Square in Glasgow for the hunger strike, a gang of BNP thugs turned up, demanding 'Where's Sheridan? We're going to get him!' His mother was there on the stall too so she got on the megaphone: 'I'm Sheridan, are you coming to get me?' When she started shouting that they were fascists in front of passers-by the BNP men turned and ran.[32] In Oldham the Anti-Poll Tax Federation had leaflets translated into Bengali and Urdu after the killing of Tahir Akram, a 14-year-old schoolboy shot in the eye by a gang of white youth in front of his younger sister. The local community was convinced it was a racist attack. Reaching out to oppressed or marginalised communities was seen as a priority.

The people's march and clashes in Brixton

In the summer of 1990, the ABAPTF began to draw up plans for how to keep the campaign in the public eye. It was essential that Poll Tax resisters across the country should know that there was a vibrant movement happening, to ensure that scattered non-payers did not feel isolated. They were cautious about calling another big protest in the autumn, partly because the Gulf War was taking up a lot of time for marches and demonstrations, partly because some were worried about another riot.

The Fed agreed to organise a People's March, based on the Jarrow march against unemployment in the 1930s, when hundreds of men marched from Jarrow to London. The plan was actually for three marches: people would set off from Manchester, Bristol and Glasgow and converge on London. Groups of people began a long trek across the country – the Glasgow leg had to cover 500 miles in six weeks – stopping off at towns and cities along the way to give talks and speeches at public meetings organised by local APTUs. Local Militant branches were expected to help organise meeting spaces and accommodation for the marchers when they entered their town. The 3D campaign complained about the organisation of the march, writing that 'the overwhelming feeling of most ordinary groups is that they were not consulted about this event'.[33] There were also complaints that the amount of resources that went into hosting a load of activists and putting on a meeting was a real strain on some smaller APTUs.

The marchers were elected at meetings of the Federation in their cities of origin. Despite a media blackout, crowds of hundreds gathered to see them off. One marcher, Sally Brown, kept a diary of her journey from Glasgow, meeting local activists and shoppers in town centres as she made her way to London. When they got to Harrogate a spread of food was laid on for them and they helped distribute some handwritten local leaflets: 'If even Harrogate has an Anti-Poll Tax campaign, how can they stop us?'[34] However, the march also showed the uneven level of engagement and organisation in different places. In Leeds they were greeted by 500 people, but a couple of days later in Barnsley there were only 'two or three interested people, no one else took a blind bit of notice!'[35] The 55 marchers were buoyed up by camaraderie and a repertoire of songs, many of them thought up on the walk.

When the marchers got to Northampton they occupied the council treasurer's office to protest the threatened imprisonment of Cyril Mundin, a 75-year-old Second World War veteran who could not afford to pay the Community Charge. The marchers went with local campaigners to the town hall and occupied it, demanding to speak to the treasurer. When he ignored them they began to barricade the office door with filing cabinets. After he left, the 20 campaigners occupied the office for most of the day, before leaving to be arrested by the police. After 24 hours in a cell and a summons to court – charged under Section 5 of the Public Order Act – they were found guilty and fined £700 each. The stunt was not worthless however; it got some press coverage and encouraged Dave Nellist, Tony Benn, Diane Abbott and Jeremy Corbyn, alongside 18 other Labour MPs, to table an early day motion in defence of Mundin. The public pressure led to the *News of the World* intervening to pay Mundin's arrears for him – patronisingly emphasising his service to the country as a war hero rather than dealing with the substance of his inability to pay an egregious tax.

When the marchers finally arrived in Kennington Park in Lambeth they were greeted by a large crowd of supporters. The final stage of the march was through Lambeth towards Brockwell Park where, while the official organisers held court on the main stage, some people took up positions at the front of the rally and 'began organised barracking of virtually every speaker', according to Militant. Sally Brown described it as a few drunks throwing beer cans at various speakers, but it was clear there was some tension within the movement between Militant and other groups.[36] Most of the cans were hurled at Nally as he tried to speak. He lamented that it was 'a waste of beer'.

A section of the protest led by the Trafalgar Square Defendants' Campaign then broke away and began a march to nearby Brixton Prison, where several people were being held on charges related to the Trafalgar Square riots. This was part of a coordinated international solidarity action, with actions happening in Amsterdam, Oslo, Athens, Melbourne, Vienna and Warsaw. The breakaway march made its way to the prison where they were intercepted by hundreds of police and contained on one side of the road. Danny Burns recalled the 'rumours flying around that the police wanted a rematch for 31 March'. As the protest went on, calling for the release of the Trafalgar Square defendants, more riot police moved into position around the demonstrators. Suddenly the mood changed and the police began pushing and shoving people. One police officer was heard shouting 'I'd like to start kicking people's heads in.' Fighting broke out as police pushed the protesters towards Brixton town centre. Local people got involved, setting up barricades using market stalls to slow the advance of the police. More police emerged from side streets; one person remembered the 'riot police ... truncheoning down anyone in their path'. The TV news that night was once again full of images of disorder in Brixton; 135 people were arrested on the day.

After the clashes Nally avoided placing any blame on the protest organisers for their breakaway and instead focused on the police's actions. But in their account of the protest published later, Militant accused Class War of behaving 'in a fashion that was totally alien to all the traditions of the working-class movement'.[37]

'Maggie Maggie Maggie, Out Out Out'

Despite the first tranche of non-payers going to prison, there was something to celebrate. Across many parts of Britain there was a mood of jubilation concerning the departure of one Margaret Thatcher. It was not one spectacular action that sealed her fate, but the slow deterioration of a government, a murmur of dissent that became a clamour for change.

Several key developments contributed to Thatcher's demise. From the mid 1980s onwards there had been a series of public sector disasters, mostly associated with transport. The Zeebrugge ferry catastrophe that claimed 196 lives,[38] the King's Cross fire, an explosion on a North Sea oil rig that killed 166, train crashes in Clapham, followed by Purley and then Glasgow – all gave the impression of a public sector infrastructure starved of cash and suffering from lax standards due to increasing dereg-ulation. Then there was the economy: inflation was topping 10 per cent again, worse than it had been when James Callaghan had been Prime Minister. This stung the Conservatives as their monetarist policies had been imposed specifically to drive inflation down. Unemployment was also creeping back up, on top of the structural unemployment that had blighted the country for the whole of the last decade. The much vaunted economic miracle had become a nightmare for many people.

On top of this there was a crisis over Britain's relationship with Europe. The question of greater integration or keeping the continent at a distance was causing serious rifts in the government, and struck right at the heart of British capitalism's strategic interests.

Clearly both the Poll Tax and relations with Europe were pressing concerns, but there was also the issue of Thatcher's electoral credibil-ity. She had decisively won the 1987 general election but the Tories had then lost the European elections in 1989 – their first national defeat since 1979. A by-election in the safe Conservative seat of Richmond, Yorkshire in February 1989 saw William Hague elected, but with a 15,000 drop in the Tory vote share. A month later Labour beat the Tories to take the Vale of Glamorgan seat. In March 1990, only a week before the Trafalgar Square riot, the Mid-Staffordshire by-election saw Labour take a safe Tory seat on a 77 per cent turnout. The winning Labour candidate, Sylvia Heal, declared the 'dark age of Thatcherism is drawing to a close'. At a by-election in Bootle the Labour candidate won handsomely, with the Tories suffering an 11 per cent swing against them. Then in Bradford North the Conservative vote plummeted by 22 per cent; this was the seat that Militant member Pat Wall had held before his death at the age of 57. A few months later the Tories had their worst ever local government election result, losing Bradford Council, though they tried to massage the defeat by heralding the fact that Wandsworth and Westminster remained true blue.

Thatcher kept a brave face on the setbacks, arguing that 'the Com-munity Charge is beginning to work. It will increasingly bring the profligate and the inefficient to book.'[39] Behind the scenes, however, she had by this time no real loyalists and few reliable people around her. Her political differences with Chancellor Lawson had been an open wound regularly prodded in the press and on the backbenches. In a spectacular error of judgement she hired an economic advisor who clashed with Lawson, leading to the latter's resignation. His replacement, John Major, then worked with other pro-European Tories to take Britain into the Exchange Rate Mechanism, partly behind Thatcher's back. She was obsessive about potential plots to remove her, and the 1987 election campaign had proven to be a huge strain, leading to a falling out with her previously loyal colleague Norman Tebbit.

One final fatal blow was the Liberal Democrat victory in the Eastbourne by-election, overturning a 16,000 Tory majority to win in the seat that had been Ian Gow's. Gow had been Thatcher's close friend until an IRA car bomb ended his life outside Parliament in July 1990. That the party could lose in a safe seat after the incumbent had been assassinated convinced nervous Tory MPs to finally make their move. Michael Heseltine wrote to his constituency chairman to sound out the possibility of standing against the Prime Minister. The letter was purposefully leaked to the press to check the public mood for such an action.

In mid-November 1990, the BBC showed the first episode of the seminal *House of Cards*, starring Ian Richardson as the dastardly and scheming Francis Urquhart. The TV show depicted the manoeuvring and even murderous duplicity of Tories scrambling for power. In the opening scene of the first episode Urquhart sits in his study, looking wistfully at a picture of Thatcher before muttering 'nothing lasts forever'. Turning to the camera with a mischievous grin, he confides in the viewer, 'even the longest, most glittering reign must come to an end some day', before placing the photo face down on his desk. On 13 November Alan Clarke MP recorded in his diaries: 'The Party is virtually out of control. Mutinous. People are not turning up for divisions. Dissidents get bolder and bolder with their little off the cuff TV slotettes. Code is abandoned. Discipline is breaking down.'[40] Thatcher had lost the one thing that all leaders utterly rely upon, her authority.

There had already been a leadership contest in December 1989, when the stalking-horse candidate Anthony Meyer challenged her. Thatcher easily swotted him aside, but 60 of her MPs did not back her, either by voting for Meyer or spoiling their ballots. That number was too high for someone of her stature. It set alarm bells ringing for her backers and intensified the bubbling mutiny among the others. The people who had been cajoling Meyer to stand had drawn blood. Pro-European Geoffrey Howe was moved from the Foreign Office to Deputy Leader after expressing his frustration and anger at Thatcher's growing Euro-scepticism. After Thatcher spoke a little too directly in Parliament about her disdain for European political integration, Howe felt compelled to resign. His resignation speech in Parliament on 1 November was a very public and very direct attack on Thatcher's government, her leadership style and her anti-European bias. He pointed to 'the tragic conflict of loyalties' facing Tory MPs. How much longer would they put personal loyalty to Thatcher ahead of the European project or their own seats (in the event of a Labour landslide at the next election)? This was especially significant as Howe had been the last remaining member of Thatcher's first government in 1979, the last man standing after a decade of turbulent politics.

Shortly after this very public exposure of the cracks at the heart of the Conservative government, Michael Heseltine, by this time a bona fide nemesis of the Prime Minister, finally broke ranks and declared his bid for the leadership. He was beaten in the first round with 152 votes to Thatcher's 204. She may have won, but it was not by enough. Most of her Cabinet trooped into her office one by one and advised her not to contest a second round.

On 26 November research was published revealing that 90 per cent of people did not agree with the Poll Tax.[41] A day later, sitting in her study, Thatcher finally accepted that her options had been reduced to only one – resignation. After a decade in power – with her near total political hegemony, her statesman-like success in defeating the powerful trade unions and local government militants, and her reshaping of attitudes that would last for generations – she had been ignobly defeated by her own side. Friendly fire brought her down. 'It's a funny old world' she murmured with tears in her eyes. The photo of her being driven to Buckingham Palace to hand in her resignation to the Queen was a lamentable end to a titan of the postwar Tory Party. But then there are no friends in politics.

It is indicative of the tenacity of the Conservative Party at the time that they succeeded in losing such a beloved leader and moving on without seeming to even look back. In part thanks to Labour pinning so much of the blame on Thatcher, many of the Conservatives and their intellectual allies who had pioneered the Poll Tax continued to have long careers in politics. As the journalist Michael Crick noted, 'The main proponents of the Poll Tax, who invented it well before Mrs Thatcher gave her stamp of approval, managed to escape unscathed. Indeed what is so remarkable is how easily several of them have progressed to higher jobs in government.'[42] William Waldegrave, who had convened the working group that fleshed out the Poll Tax proposal and recommended it to Thatcher at the infamous meeting at Chequers, was one of the unscathed. He later wrote in his memoirs that there was little pressure on him to resign. 'It was relatively easy for me to defend myself: "What? Do you really think one lowly parliamentary under-secretary in the Department of Education could have orchestrated something like that? Ridiculous!"'[43]

By December the Tories had overtaken Labour in the polls again, a serious turnaround from the summer when Labour had been favourites to win an election.

Given how despised Thatcher was in working-class communities, there were spontaneous street parties in some parts of Britain. People gathered in pubs to drink and cheer the downfall of the Iron Lady. Brian Smedley in Bridgwater immediately went to the local court to announce the good news: 'Bridgwater Magistrates Court was where the latest victims of the Poll Tax were being summonsed, fined or imprisoned for non-payment. The Anti-Poll Tax Union was there as always to support them. I burst into the courtroom and shouted the news of Thatcher's resignation. APTU members cheered. Allan Challenger, a solid activist throughout the campaign, stood up and pointed at the magistrates shouting "Your leader's gone now its time for YOU to go!"'

8

Endgame

'From today, therefore, taxes are abolished! It is high treason to pay taxes.
Refusal to pay taxes is the primary duty of the citizen!'

Karl Marx

The second All Britain Anti-Poll Tax Federation conference was held in November 1990, at the Apollo Theatre in Manchester. The movement was in good spirits after the protests and the sheer scale of non-payment was still obvious. The conference was still largely dominated by Militant delegates from the local groups – they were given a different agenda to the other attendees, which indicated which way to vote on all the key issues: oppose, support, refer.

Inevitably there were repercussions from the 31 March protest. One motion from the Lewisham APTU condemned 'the statements made by the Chair and Secretary of the All Britain Anti-Poll Tax Federation blaming demonstrators and political groups for the violence instigated by the police, and offering to "name names"'. Furthermore, it called on the conference to disassociate itself from the Fed's 'cowardly refusal to organise further mass demonstrations, as shown by its hostility to the call for a mass demonstration in London on October 20th'. The agenda for Militant members simply noted: OPPOSE.[1]

Beyond these ructions however, the campaign against the bailiffs was producing serious results. Councils were finding it almost impossible to get back the money that was owed them. Since the councils were having trouble using the bailiffs, the government advised them simply to seek court orders to have the money removed directly from people's wages – known as wage arrestment. This meant issuing Attachment of Earnings Orders to employers and taking the money straight from the tax-refuser's pay packet to send to the local council.

The Fed argued that employers should appeal against the wage arrestments, since possible strike action by their staff might end up costing them more than they would spend on the arrestment: 'an employer faced with the prospect of losing millions of pounds in lost production through threatened strike action could turn around to the courts and the council and tell them that it is impractical to deduct Poll Tax arrears from wages. This factor backs up the effectiveness of waging industrial action against the threat of wage arrestments.'[2]

There were several major problems with using wage arrestments. The first was that the council did not know where everyone worked, and getting that information using snoopers or by cross-referencing files was expensive and time consuming. Even when they did find out where people worked, many employers proved unhelpful. Processing the arrestments took a lot of effort; indeed, the human resources trade magazine *Personnel Today* described it as 'payroll havoc'. Another problem was that people owed hundreds of pounds, but arrestments of earnings were capped, limited to a maximum of £9 per week for someone earning £100 a week or £1.85 for a single person on benefits. This meant that only £95 could be recovered from someone on benefits per year. In the end only a handful of companies introduced wage arrestments, mainly in the South West: the civil service in Devon, Cornwall and Avon took money from their employees' wages, as did the bus company in Bristol and Rolls Royce Contractors. Many employers openly stated they were worried that wage arrestments would undermine industrial relations with their employees, and lobbied the government to only use the measure as 'a last resort'.[3]

In Scotland Council's had the power to freeze the bank accounts of refuseniks, which led to a series of creative and ingenious methods designed to frustrate the authorities. These included making subtle changes to names so they differed from those on the Poll Tax computer, changing the correspondence address of the bank account, moving accounts to a smaller bank or putting money into a child's bank account. The technical capacity to take money from people's wages or bank accounts was simply not in place, and a really determined Poll Tax resister could tie up council officials in hours of investigations and paperwork that even then might not deliver much of the money owed. The big banks themselves were also weary of assisting the courts in freezing accounts, fearing it might drive their customers away. And there was an additional very basic problem in that around 30 per cent of adults in Britain did not have a bank account in 1989.

Nevertheless, in Scotland, Labour councils moved to dock the income support of non-payers. Internal documents were leaked to the Fed showing that Strathclyde Council was docking the benefits of over

13,000 people.[4] The head of finance in the region had sent over 50,000 names to the DSS to get the money taken directly from their income support. This was the equivalent of £2.30 a week, the cost of a hot meal. It was this targeted attack on 'the poorest people in the poorest area in Western Europe' that led Sheridan and several others to organise the hunger strike in George Square.[5]

In 1990 the Poll Tax in Wandsworth was set at £136, but neighbouring Lambeth taxed its residents £560. This discrepancy allowed the Conservatives to claim that a well-run and efficient Tory council like Wandsworth would lead to a cheaper Community Charge, whereas a wasteful Labour-run council like Lambeth would have to rinse their residents for cash for frivolous projects like 'police monitoring' or self-defence classes for lesbians. This played well in the media, with journalists taking the opportunity to do vox pops on a street bordering the two boroughs to compare and contrast the costs of living. Behind the propaganda, though, lay the reality of Wandsworth as a privatising council that had slashed local services since the 1970s and enjoyed special discretionary grants that boosted their coffers. Even other Tory councils would look jealously on Wandsworth's special status as 'Margaret Thatcher's favourite borough'.

As Thatcher's successor John Major was settling into the role of Prime Minister, his government fought desperately to buy some time to save the tax. In January 1991 they announced a Community Charge reduction scheme and maintained local government funds at the enhanced level that had been agreed by Patten the previous summer. In the next budget, Major's government took the drastic step of reducing the Community Charge bill arbitrarily by £140 per person in a desperate attempt to save the policy. This was no generous refund, however, since it was paid for by an increase in VAT from 15 per cent to 17.5 per cent – another form of regressive taxation that was not based on ability to pay and hit poorer consumers the most. When the Chancellor Norman Lamont announced the £140 reduction it came as a huge surprise, even to Tory councils. The Poll Tax collection department in Bradford had been ready to work through the night to prepare the bills for dispatch – when the news came through later that evening, they were sent home as every single bill had to be pulped and recalculated. The cut also led to the curious situation where Wandsworth residents had a Poll Tax bill of zero – in fact, since Wandsworth charged £136 per head, technically the council owed each resident £4.

Kinnock rebuked the inept last-ditch efforts of the government to save the Community Charge as merely throwing more good money after a bad policy: 'what we haven't got from all of the cost and chaos is a single additional home help, not a single extra police officer, not an extra teacher or road repair'.[6]

Just as Labour had suffered an upset at the Govan by-election in 1988, it was now the Conservatives' turn. The constituency of Ribble Valley was vacated by David Waddington, who had been Home Secretary during the Poll Tax riot and was quietly removed and elevated to the Lords by Major for his failures. Ribble Valley was one of the safest Tory seats in the country, with a 20,000 majority. But after a concerted campaign the Liberal Democrats took the seat with a 5,000 majority in March 1991. The defeat was significant. The British government had just helped win the war in Iraq and were hoping for a Falklands-style boost, but the defeat in Ribble Valley sent the hares running as the Tories searched for excuses – or scapegoats. The Liberal Democrats had put the Poll Tax front and centre in their campaign, counterposing it to their call for a local income tax. For Major, the Tory rout demonstrated that it was not enough to have replaced Thatcher or reformed the Community Charge – it had to be scrapped.

By this stage the Community Charge was in a vicious circle. A provision of the policy which proved fatal was that charges would be increased annually to make up for shortfalls in previous years. This created a situation where those people who were paying the tax would end up with higher bills as increasing numbers of their neighbours boycotted it. Inevitably this had the effect of encouraging those who had previously been law abiding to join the boycott instead of seeing their annual bill soar.

The ability of councils to enforce the tax diminished as bailiff and sheriff firms started to go bankrupt. Hoping for a windfall from collecting the tax, the firms had hired numerous additional staff, but having recovered very little money most of them subsequently lost a fortune. Macclesfield Council, for instance, revealed that their bailiffs had collected only 7 per cent of the tax owed.[7] Guildford had collected only £11 million of the £35 million it was owed; Haringey just £12 million of the £46 million owed. Stories in the papers about the excesses of desperate bailiffs began to increase. In one notable incident, Caroline Rockey from Tiverton was confronted by two 'hefty men' who forced their way into her house and threatened to sell her dog to pay off the debt.[8]

It was only a matter of time now, yet still the councils were ruthlessly prosecuting non-payers. The number of people in prison – while steadily rising – still dwarfed the millions who were not paying or who had paid only a small amount. Nationally, the number of non-payers was growing rapidly. As the protestors chanted outside the courts: 'you can't jail us all!' The fear of prison was not working when it came to disciplining the population. There was also a financial issue with the jailings – people were being sent to prison for on average 20 days for not paying a £400 Poll Tax bill, but each day in prison was costing the government around £100 per prisoner. Mass jailings were not sustainable; they had to be used in a surgical manner to try to spread fear or to undermine campaigns by targeting the local APTU leaders.

The flagship is sunk

As tens of thousands gathered in Hyde Park in March 1991 for a protest called by the Fed, CIPFA produced a report that same month with statistical data about the level of non-payment. It was devastating. For Major, it was clear the tax was a massive problem that had to be dealt with. Much to the anger of the Thatcherites, he appointed Heseltine as Environment Secretary and put him in charge of a review into the tax. The committee of senior ministers that met behind closed doors quickly realised that more tinkering and reform was simply not going to work. As the *Financial Times* summed it up: 'Almost all agree on one thing … voters simply will not accept that the duke and the dustman should pay the same.'9 The moral economy had won.

Only days after having reduced the tax by £140 per person, on Thursday 21 March 1991 Michael Heseltine announced that the Poll Tax was to be abolished. 'An astonishing week', Benn noted in his dairy. The *Financial Times* described it as 'the most spectacular U-turn by any government this century'. But it would be another two years before the tax was replaced with the Council Tax. The new tax was based on the value of people's homes, which ostensibly was fairer than a simple flat tax but, as it was still not based on ability to pay, it remained a regressive tax. The only concession was that the homes were banded, the assumption being that poorer people lived in smaller homes. Major managed to pilot it through Parliament; Labour still had no credible alternative. Still, it was the Tories time to be in disarray and shoulder a crisis that was of their own making. One Tory MP on the Poll Tax review committee glumly admitted: 'the Conservative party are good at organising two things, memorial services and retreats. We are conducting an organised retreat under fire.'[10]

The campaign had succeeded by frustrating the implementation of the Poll Tax successfully at every stage until the cost of administering it and the sheer energy and resources required to sustain it had made it unworkable. The tax was clearly not as efficient nor as politically palatable as the rates system. Considering the point of the tax was to fund local government, it was failing in its entire purpose. It was costing more to implement than it was earning. Nearly 30 per cent of the population had been summonsed to court, liability orders had been issued against 22 per cent, and 9 per cent had been visited by bailiffs. The sheer scale of the fight with a recalcitrant population unwilling to be taxed so heavily proved too much. The flagship policy of Thatcherism had cost £1.5 billion in five years, and devoured around £20 billion in rebates. The unexpected cost was so heavy that it trigged inflation in the economy, something that critics of the tax had warned of. Hugo Young called the tax 'six years of political blundering on a scale unequalled in the postwar era'.[11] Nigel Lawson, who had predicted that the tax would be 'completely unworkable and politically catastrophic', was proven right.

'Extra-parliamentary action, that nightmare of Westminster politics, proved itself … this weekend each and every one of those non-payers can feel proud of themselves', wrote *The Observer*. The *Financial Times* too conceded that the Community Charge had been 'killed by a citizens rebellion'.[12]

The Battle of Turnbull Street

But the war was not over. One of the last big public battles over the Poll Tax came with the attempt to carry out the first warrant sale of impounded goods in Scotland. This event on 1 October 1991 became known as the Battle of Turnbull Street. It was testimony to the strength and tenacity of the campaign that it had taken over two years for a single warrant sale to occur in Scotland; the mass opposition had simply been too strong for the sheriffs and the courts. Anticipating trouble, a judge had issued Sheridan with an interdict the day before to prevent him from going within 200 yards of the sale. The sheriff delivering the interdict had quietly crept up to Sheridan's front door and posted it through, not daring to alert Sheridan's neighbours or friends to his presence. Ignoring the judge, the next day Sheridan led a column of around 500 people to the gates of a police detention centre in East Glasgow. Alongside Sheridan marched Janet McGinn, the first woman fined under the Poll Tax, along with many other comrades and allies she had met during the course of the last two-and-a-half years.

The compound was protected by large wrought-iron gates which the demonstrators grappled with until eventually they tore them down and poured inside. They were met by hundreds of police armed with truncheons and riot shields who poured out of cars and minibuses and surrounded the sheriff's van. There was a scuffle before the sheer numbers filled the space and the police pulled back slightly, but remained a wall of yellow and black, keeping a watchful eye. Sheridan jumped up on top of a nearby barrier and shouted 'Look folk its all cool in here ... our fight is not with the police, we are here to protest about the scum who are carrying out the barbaric practice of selling off this woman's household goods.'[13] He then tore up the piece of paper with the interdict on. 'I am not prepared to stand back and watch this barbarism take place. We are warning the police now that as soon as these goods are released from the back of the van, then I, and I believe I am speaking for everyone here, will do everything in my power to prevent this sale taking place.'[14]

After a tense stand-off the warrant sale was cancelled and the demonstrators dispersed, cheering and chanting. A victory for the movement, but Sheridan had exposed himself to arrest with his public flaunting of a court order.

Scottish Militant Labour

For Militant, the Poll Tax movement was the height of their influence and political profile. They had embraced the strategy of non-payment when the rest of the left still looked to the unions as the key force for social resistance. They had led a mass movement. But the campaign had also changed them politically. They had done far less Labour Party work, many members had stopped going to their ward and CLP meetings, mainly because all their time was taken up with the APTUs. As Militant organiser Rob Sewell explained: 'Our mass work around the Poll Tax placed colossal pressure on the comrades, especially in the localities, and the burden, which was increasing, was falling on fewer and fewer shoulders. We were beginning to fall victim to the limitations of "single issue" politics and the work was becoming more and more unbalanced. This had very negative consequences.'[15] Labour Party structures were either totally absent or – where they did engage – proved to be a drag on local mobilisations. On top of this, prominent members had been expelled during the campaign. In Scotland several Militant members had been purged in a witch-hunt led by the ex-chair of Stop It, Brian Wilson. In England, Terry Fields and Dave Nellist were expelled. In response, at the 1991 Labour Party conference, Jeremy Corbyn led a march of 5,000 people around the hall in support of Fields and Nellist. It was also noted wryly that *The Spectator* had just awarded Nellist 'backbencher of the year', partly for his work challenging the Poll Tax. Steve Nally was suspended then expelled for his membership of Militant and public Anti-Poll Tax activities, as were several other Militant members nationally.

Faced with expulsions and a significant threat to their organisation, the remaining members of Militant in Scotland formally left Labour, founding Scottish Militant Labour in October 1991. They castigated Labour for its failures as a social democratic reformist party. From his own perspective, Sheridan, having already been expelled himself, 'found it increasingly difficult to stick to the original message of my speeches: urging people to join Labour and change it from within'.[16] The flat contradiction of attempting to reform the Labour Party as their cadre were being expelled from it and APTU activists were being barred entry (even if they were not in Militant), left the tendency with an apparently inoperable strategy. In addition, the Labour Party Young Socialists, which was dominated by Militant, had been effectively closed down when the NEC reduced the maximum age from 27 to 21, excluding most of the young Militant leaders from the organisation. There seemed to be little left for Militant to remain in Labour.

After an internal debate, it was decided that the organisation should be divided, with the English and Welsh sections remaining in Labour and the Scottish section leaving to reconstitute itself in time to stand in the 1992 general election. They wanted Tommy Sheridan to stand in Pollok – but there was a problem.

Sheridan in Saughton

For his actions in preventing the warrant sale on Turnbull Street, Sheridan received his summons to court. Sheridan now took his place alongside the other martyrs of the campaign – perhaps the biggest prize of them all for the authorities. He was convicted in the Supreme Court in

Edinburgh for breaking the interdict. This was the same Supreme Court where stewards from the Clyde Workers Committee had been sent into exile in 1916 and where the Calton Weavers had been sentenced to being whipped through the street.[17]

Sheridan's defence was that he was protecting a vulnerable older woman whose goods had been seized. While this was a moral defence it was not a legal one. The judge sentenced him to prison for six months, provoking gasps among some of his supporters in the courtroom. 'We'll be back' he said as he was led away, although he wished he'd said something more memorable. Sheridan was taken to Saughton Prison and put in the cells. He received a generally warm welcome from the other convicts who shook their heads and agreed that he should never have been sent down.

While in prison Sheridan ran as the Scottish Militant Labour candidate for the parliamentary seat in Pollok. In the minds of the prison authorities this granted him something akin to political prisoner status. He was moved to a better cell and given access to an early type of mobile phone to organise his campaign from the prison. His confinement meant the campaigning had to be done for him by comrades speaking on his behalf, but it gave Sheridan a notoriety and a unique selling point: elect the man who had been imprisoned for fighting the Poll Tax. Sheridan considered himself to be in the same vein as people like Eugene Debs, the US socialist who had run for president while in prison in 1920; John McClean who ran for MP from a prison cell in 1918; and even Bobby Sands, the first person to run for a seat in the British Parliament and win while incarcerated. Sheridan's manifesto was launched from a prison hall and several press conferences were held there during the campaign. In the event, he came second, with 6,287 votes as against the 14,170 for Labour. Within a few months Sheridan stood again in the Regional District elections, this time winning a seat in his hometown of Pollok. He was released from prison in the summer of 1992.

Unfinished business

The Local Government Finance Act 1992 – which replaced the Community Charge with the Council Tax – received Royal Assent on 6 March that year. The Poll Tax was officially dead, but it would not be replaced with the new system until 1 January 1993. The campaign had to sustain itself – the tax was still being charged and councils were still pursuing people for their money. In defeat the Poll Tax was like a dying animal lashing out even more violently. The first six months of 1991 saw the number of people going to prison rise dramatically. The same month that Heseltine made his statement, Thanet Council had four residents in the docks for non-payment. One was sent to prison and three others were given a suspended sentence. One, Jimmy Haddow, continued to refuse to pay so was summoned to serve prison time. The local APTU organised a hunger strike in solidarity. Haddow was sentenced on 2 May – the day of the local elections. Labour won the vote and replaced the Tories, meaning he spent his first day in prison under a Labour administration. He remembered that the activists 'heard through the grapevine later that the Labour leadership were furious that the hunger strike took place because they thought it would scupper their vote'. Days after his release, his then wife Ruby Haddow – a mother of three children with no income – was sent to Holloway prison for non-payment.

Kim Larke was summoned to court for a £70 unpaid Poll Tax bill. He was unemployed and had experienced a period of homelessness in the mid 1980s. In court he was questioned extensively about his finances: 'the Broadland Council representative was merely trying to establish that my failure to pay was a refusal rather than an inability to pay. To be fair it was a mixture of both. I was living on a meagre income but I was fiercely opposed to the Poll Tax.' He was sent down for ten days, whisked away to prison without any friends knowing where he was. Without his anxiety medication he was scared of having a panic attack. Upon his arrival he found that the prison authorities also seemed to think his incarceration was a waste of their time. After 10 days he was released; 'I was given a letter to take down to the DHSS. I was given a large amount of money in the form of a giro. I was being given money from the government for going to prison for owing the government money.'[18]

Still the problems continued. With less than a year to go until the new Council Tax, it transpired that nearly 200 councils had been using faulty software to issue their summonses. A computer error had added two years' worth of summonses together into a single payment demand, which was illegal under the law. This required entire batches to be withdrawn, and led to even more frustration in courts when judges had to throw out whole days of work because of mistakes by the councils' computers. Lambeth, Brent, Havering, Southwark and Camden all reported problems. One magistrate, Mr Justin Philips, was infuriated with the number of mistakes from Lambeth Council. A catalogue of errors culminated in a summons for the wrong amount to a Mr Evans. The judge exploded with rage at the legal representative from Lambeth: 'If you have persuaded me to issue one liability order wrongly, then you have corrupted my system.' He quashed all the liability orders granted and instructed the council to send 4,000 letters of apology within seven days. Unable to locate the court reporter he asked the APTU activist from Streatham, Graham Lewis – acting as a McKenzie friend – to record the judgement so it could be raised in Parliament.

One of the final and most devastating legal setbacks came early in 1992 when Lawyers Against the Poll Tax successfully argued that the computer evidence was inadmissible. They had been challenging the lawfulness of this evidence since the summer of 1990, on the grounds that council officers who relied on computer print-outs of financial details to help secure liability orders had no first-hand knowledge of people's debts – the computer evidence was second-hand information. Because the magistrates courts were made up of lay judges they were often too quick to accept the probative value of computer evidence.[19] Lawyers pointed out that because the computer data had been inputted by one council worker and was being read out in court by another, the latter had no way of knowing for sure that the original data was correct. They might have a computer print-out in front of them, but who could say whether or not human error had corrupted that information? As such, the claim that someone owed money to the council was simply hearsay. After Mr Christopher Bourke, the Clerkenwell stipendiary magistrate, ruled that this was a legally sound argument, and it was confirmed in the case of *Coventry Justices ex p Bullard* (1992), over 250,000 liability orders were thrown out across the country, forcing the government to scramble to close the legal loophole.

Despite the victory of the movement against the tax, Kinnock was determined to continue to use the campaign as an excuse to purge the ranks of his own party. All the Labour members on the national committee of the ABAPTF were suspended. Party General Secretary Larry Whitty was unrepentant: 'The party had to be seen to be taking action in London against the Left.' Other disciplinary actions were taken against left-wingers in Nottingham and St Helens, and another investigation was opened up into members in Liverpool. Only two people on the NEC opposed these actions, Tony Benn and Dennis Skinner. Skinner lamented that the party was attacking its own members instead of the Tories, just at the point when the government was in retreat on the Poll

Tax.[20] The venom of the Labour right nevertheless persisted and the party was, till the end, loyally implementing the tax despite the mass protests and the social chaos it was causing.

The party bureaucracy ensured where possible that Anti-Poll Tax campaigners did not stand as candidates for Parliament. After the Tory MP Ian Gow was assassinated by the IRA, the local Labour Party in Eastbourne selected their only Labour councillor, Peter Day, who had publicly campaigned against the tax. Much to their shock they were overruled by Labour HQ, who instead imposed Charlotte Atkins, the then head of the Labour group from Wandsworth.[21]

In the same month the Community Charge was formally declared to be on life support, Lambeth Council leader Joan Twelves and several allies were suspended by Labour's NEC for bringing the party into disrepute. One charge against them was their decision not to use bailiffs to collect the Poll Tax. Twelves and councillor John Harrison were accused of 'advocating non-enforcement of the tax' and 'non-payment of the tax' – referring to an internal circular in the Labour group which recommended supporting those councillors who were refusing to pay their tax as a matter of principle or conscience. The Labour right condemned the left on Lambeth Council for their 'cynical tactics' of taking the council 'to the brink of illegality, refusing to implement measures such as Poll Tax collection and enforcement'. This would force finance officers to bring Section 114 notices to the council – threatening surcharge. The left could then rely on opposition councillors and the Labour right to vote through measures to prevent the surcharge, allowing the left to retain their oppositional status, 'secure in the knowledge that others were doing their dirty work for them'.[22]

Labour councils made more cuts in the run up to the 1992 election, many of them publicly blaming non-payment for their financial problems, even though by the end only a small part of their budget relied on income from the Community Charge. Blaming non-payers and aggressively pursuing them to the point of imprisonment only diverted blame from the Tories onto Labour's own electorate, who were fighting to resist a tax that the Labour Party itself had agreed was iniquitous.

Between the announcement that the Poll Tax would be scrapped and the 1992 election, Labour was caught in a terrible bind. The local tax bills were still astronomical but their councillors were committed to collection. They decided to double down on attacking the non-payment movement. The imprisonment of non-payers by Labour councils was becoming such an issue that Collyhurst Tenants association called for a lobby of the Labour NEC over the jailings in February 1992.

Even in relation to the continued persecution of tax resisters using the new computer systems, Labour positively goaded the government to improve the rates of conviction. Bryan Gould, the Shadow Environment Minister, offered the government Labour support to rush through a controversial bill that would close the loophole on computer evidence, making it admissible as well as applicable retrospectively to enable a greater conviction rate. He defended Labour's position by saying that 'lazy and incompetent' government was letting people get away with non-payment.[23] This would have been a prime opportunity for Labour to drive the nails deeper into the coffin; instead they positioned themselves as the 'loyal opposition'.

On 25 February 1992, it was reported that 167 people had been jailed in the last 15 months in relation to the tax. By this point 60 out of over 400 councils, several of them Labour controlled, had sent someone to jail. Burnley Council was particularly keen to incarcerate, sending 23 people to prison. Nally remembered the magistrates as being almost medieval in their attitudes. It was noted that one of the bench in Burnley who was handing out the prison sentences had stood as a Conservative councillor at the 1991 local elections – leading to a serious challenge in the court as to its supposed objectivity.

The jailings were sometimes targeted at chairs or secretaries of the APTUs, as well as well-known socialists or trade unionists. Others appeared almost random – people with no political affiliation at all were sentenced, the very old were hauled before judges, unemployed men were sent to prison. In fact, fewer people were jailed during the Poll Tax years than they were on average under the rates system, but due to the politically charged nature of the tax each imprisonment became a campaign, with each name emblazoned on leaflets and posters for solidarity gigs. The Fed organised a national amnesty conference on 15 February 1992 to keep the issue of Poll Tax prisoners in the media and encourage support for them. People joined protests across Europe calling for the release of the prisoners; 100 protestors clashed with riot police outside the UK embassy in Paris. In Canada, anarchists were chased through the streets by police during a visit by Prince Charles and Lady Diana, after unfurling a banner with the slogan AMNESTY FOR POLL TAX PRISONERS.

A month later there was the annual protest march in Glasgow, smaller this time, but nonetheless it was a celebration. Thatcher was gone, the Poll Tax was dead. A rare but cherished moment of victory.

Wilful and culpable

The Fed had been calling for an amnesty for all Poll Tax refusers, but the defeat of Labour at the 1992 election meant that there was no immediate chance of that. There had been a debt write off for British Telecom and the gas and water boards prior to their privatisation to make them more palatable for investors, but such a courtesy was not extended to the millions of non-payers of the Community Charge. Although the Fed appealed to the government to send instructions to all local authorities to remit the debt of those unable to pay – which they had the power to do – this fell on deaf ears.

By this stage, most left-wing politicians, whether they were councillors or MPs, had paid their debts, as had celebrities and the better-off. The left Labour councillors argued that for them non-payment was a political act – they did not actively want to deprive local authorities of money, so they settled their debts. Some councillors who had been elected on an Anti-Poll Tax platform were issued with a committal order for prison but paid the debt in full before sentencing. The poorest people who could not pay remained at the mercy of the courts, facing fines and even imprisonment. The legacy of imprisonment inflicted on many vulnerable people by their councils after the Community Charge had been scrapped was a blight in many areas.

In many ways, those who were targeted for non-payment after 1993 suffered more, as the movement had effectively wound up by late 1992. The volunteer army of McKenzie friends had vanished and the local APTUs had stopped meeting. This lack of support left Poll Tax debtors worse off than criminals, as they were denied legal aid or an appeal. Although the legal system is often weighted against the poor, either through outright unjust laws or because justice is meted out by people from particular class backgrounds, sometimes prominent legal battles can produce crusading fighters for justice from within the system. It was left up to a small group of young left-wing lawyers – including Alan Murdie, Keir Starmer and Liz Davies – to fight for them in the courts. They found themselves facing barristers like Cherie Booth QC, prosecuting the poor on behalf of councils, who was arguing for penniless debtors to be imprisoned.[24]

Another valiant barrister fighting on behalf of non-payers was Richard Wise. Wise was still active in trying to get people out of prison, particularly those sent down for debt. In 1995 he represented 161 Poll Tax defaulters, mainly women, and had a good success rate in keeping them out of prison. In a survey of the Poll Tax prisoners, Rona Epstein and Richard Wise found that while only ten people had been jailed for non-payment in 1990/1, the number had sky-rocketed to 704 the following year and increased again to 1,202 between March 1993 to March 1994. Even more concerning, the sentences were getting longer. Many of these cases in the latter years were imprisonment for poverty. Nearly 150 people applied for judicial review to the High Court and were successful in over 90 per cent of cases – this was almost unprecedented as the average success rate was only 15 per cent. Magistrates were imprisoning people for non-payment who were on income support or other benefits, had no income, had serious mental or physical disabilities, or were suffering serious illnesses that made it hard for them to hold down steady jobs.[25]

The legal argument over imprisonment was largely one of proportionality. The threat of prison was one option open to councils to reclaim debt, but they had to make a reasonable case that it was proportionate given the circumstances. Michael Howard had declared in Parliament in 1988 that 'Imprisonment applies only where there is a deliberate non-payment and where the person has the moneys with which to pay.' The lawyers had to prove 'wilful refusal' or 'culpable neglect' in not paying. This view was redolent of the Victorian distinction between the deserving and the undeserving poor; essentially the council had to prove that someone had been feckless with their money, and this was different from someone who was simply too poor to pay. This led to some very personal court scenes where a defendant's private life was raked over to find evidence that they were in debt through their own wilful negligence.

One of those who had their sentence overturned by the High Court was Stephen Benham, a 28 year old from Poole who was imprisoned because he had quit his job and therefore his inability to pay the tax was deemed to be a result of 'culpable neglect'. The argument was made that because he had several O Levels, there was no legitimate reason for him not to be in work. Like other Poll Tax prisoners, Benham was denied legal aid, even though he was facing a committal order. The human rights campaign group Liberty took Benham's trial as a test case all the way to the European Commission of Human Rights in Strasbourg and won, leading to a ruling from the European judges that the UK government was in breach of Article 5 of the European Human Rights Convention and had to allow legal aid if the debtor was being threatened with prison. This caused much anger back in Westminster and the Tory government began to look for more ways to loosen the grip of the Strasbourg judges on UK law.

The imprisonments were particularly unjust and illogical as they were intended to be a means to secure payment. But by the mid 1990s the vast majority of people who were on trial for non-payment were simply unable to pay. The cost of imprisonment meant sending someone to prison for 28 days for owing £350 in unpaid Poll Tax was financially self-defeating. Nevertheless it continued to happen. By this time Poll Tax debtors were in court alongside people who had not paid their TV licence, another flat-rate tax that some people simply could not afford. In cases were the debt was paid it was not unusual for the debtor to get the money from a loan shark – meaning that their duty was discharged as far as the state was concerned but it could lead to spiralling levels of poverty and intimidation from dangerous criminals.

In August 1994, over a year after the Community Charge was replaced, people were still being threatened with prison for historic fines. During that year, over 1,100 people were sentenced to prison as councils struggled to try and collect the £1.75 billion that had not been paid, either through poverty or wilful political opposition.[26] One non-payer was Adele Cooper, a 22 year old who had got into arrears in the final year of the tax and owed £400. Stafford Borough Council sent her to prison despite her protestations of poverty. As the *Legal Gazette* sadly noted: 'Many of those involved either with the Anti-Poll Tax campaign or just with those who had difficulty in paying the bills saw our system of justice in action for the first time and were left with a very poor opinion of it.'[27]

It was not until 1999 in England and Wales that the billions in uncollected Poll Tax were finally written off. Under Regulation 438 of the Community Charge Administration and Enforcement Regulations 1989, there was a six-year statute of limitation on issuing liability orders; the last ones had gone out in January 1993. Finally in 2014, the Scottish government wrote off £450 million in unpaid debt related to the Community Charge. Alex Salmond MSP announced that, 'After 25 years, it's about time that the Poll Tax was finally dead and buried in Scotland.'[28]

9
Social Movements, Class and Strategy

PART I

Did the mass movement stop the tax?

The history of the Poll Tax raises a series of useful political questions. We can start with the argument that the grassroots campaign against it was not decisive in defeating the tax. The idea that 'non-payment … on its own played a fairly insignificant role in the downfall of the tax' is one that Andrew Adonis, Tony Travers and David Butler put forward in their 1994 book.[1] Their argument is that it was primarily a failure of government policy, not the consequence of a mass movement. A similar position has even been repeated by some on the Labour left more recently. 'Acid Corbynism' advocate Jeremy Gilbert, for instance, has claimed that 'The Anti-Poll-Tax campaign was only strong in areas that were always safe Labour strongholds, and as such had no effect whatsoever on Tory government policy, which was reversed not because of the APTU but because middle-income swing voters in marginal constituencies with low property values, and consequently low council rates, particularly in the North-West and the West Midlands, were suddenly seeing their tax bill go up and were very unhappy about it.'[2]

But as we have seen there were organised Anti-Poll Tax Unions in several traditional Tory areas. Such meetings and networks of local people agitating against payment contributed to the general sense that the Poll Tax was deeply unpopular, even in more Conservative areas. A mass protest and high levels of non-payment in places like Tunbridge Wells led one commentator to note: 'I knew Thatcher was done for when I read that according to official figures a third of the people of Tunbridge Wells are not paying.'[3] Across the south coast there were active APTUs and their impact didn't go unnoticed. In his autobiography Heseltine wrote that the political trauma of the Poll Tax 'did not merely surface in traditional areas of agitation, like Glasgow or Lambeth or Trafalgar

Square. Across the home counties and even in the broad acres of remote areas like Shropshire good Tory voters packed protest meetings as they had never done before.'[4]

The claim of commentators like Gilbert and Adonis rests on the belief that there was no real connection between the mass non-payment campaign and the spectacular collapse of electoral support for the Tories in by-elections in 1990. However, it would be a mistake to underestimate the role that the movement played in influencing the views of wider society. Without the mass movement – one that educated, demonstrated and solidified public opinion against the tax, turning individual complainants into an organised social force – how much of a swing would have occurred in those by-elections? It was precisely the delegitimisation of the tax through concerted political opposition that created the conditions for the wider electoral problems for the government.

An academic study found that while there was a higher rate of Poll Tax non-compliance among the unemployed and lower paid, this also occurred in Conservative-controlled local authorities, suggesting a 'greater use of non-compliance in such cases as a means of political protest against the Conservative party who introduced the tax'.[5] 'Non-compliance' here could refer either to the people who could pay but *refused* to or to those who could *probably* pay but only if they made savings elsewhere – the squeezed middle. The researchers also found that knowing your neighbours were not paying would boost non-compliance as it overcame feelings of social stigma or guilt over breaking the law. This points again to the importance of a non-payment movement which exposed isolated individuals to the knowledge that there were others in the country in a similar situation and also taking action by refusing to pay.

The argument of Adonis et al. that it was primarily a failure of political process ignores the manner in which the tax collapsed. Their conclusion is that a better class of politician would never have allowed the Poll Tax debacle to happen. While it was clearly badly handled, the governmental process alone would not have guaranteed that the Community Charge failed; after all, people have often lived with iniquitous laws for many years before they were eventually removed from the statute books. The institutional failure certainly created a lot of the problems that affected the Community Charge, but it is entirely conceivable that with some minor alterations the tax could in essence have been retained for years.

The conclusions drawn by Adonis and his co-authors are rooted in a social democratic aversion to mass protest as a means of effecting social change. Those who identify mostly with the Labour tradition will also be prone to underestimate the impact of the non-payment campaign, since their natural predilection is to see politics as something that primarily happens only in Parliament or at election time. Because they understand politics as a process that takes place mostly through the parliamentary system, they will inevitably downplay the role of a mass civil disobedience campaign in defeating an unjust law.

Labour problems

As we have seen, the record of Labour's role in the Anti-Poll Tax movement makes for grim reading. It is telling that the Labour right's main line of attack against the left was that they were guilty of 'gesture politics', when they themselves were reduced to tokenistic or rhetorical opposition at best, and were actively jailing campaigners at worst. Was this just a product of a particularly right-wing leadership under Kinnock or something more institutional, something embedded in the DNA of the party?

Labour exists in an ambiguous political space as a parliamentary party that relies on the support of trade unions, organisations that are capable of carrying out extra-parliamentary action to effect political change if they so desire. In a period when the Labour leadership was trying to distance itself from striking workers on picket lines and local government resistance in places like Liverpool and Lambeth, it doubled down on its opposition to civil disobedience in order to reinforce its status as a legitimate party of government.

Within Labour there has always been a tension between the wing of the party oriented and integrated into the British state and the radical left who are more sceptical of the state and keen to engage in political and industrial struggles outside of the usual electoral arithmetic of liberal democracy.[6] Most people will accept that some degree of protest is legitimate, a peaceful demonstration to register discontent with a government policy for instance. The reality, however, is that very few government policies are ever stopped through peaceful protests, particularly if the government is itself strongly ideologically motivated.

We have seen how the official labour movement was only interested in protest marches, which even they conceded would be ineffectual because the TUC and Labour leaders implored people to wait until the 1992 general election to get rid of the tax. For their part, the trade unions were absolutely wedded to staying within the law, even through the anti-union laws of the 1980s were designed precisely to prevent any significant action by workers that might frustrate Tory policies, as had happened under Heath in the early 1970s. It is not surprising that the Labour right were keen to argue against extra-parliamentary activity, but it is notable just how extreme they were in opposing it. While the TUC called a couple of demonstrations because they felt they had to, Labour's leadership became steadfastly opposed to *all* forms of practical resistance.

This opposition came from both the concerted pressure of the New Right and their allies in the media who were keen to undermine Labour's electoral support by tarnishing the party with the brush of radical left militancy, but also from an organic aversion on the part of the social democratic right to politics outside of the controlled environment of elections. In this context, the New Right were pushing at an open door in their criticisms of the Labour left, since Kinnock was only too willing to use the Poll Tax movement as an excuse to purge his party of left-wingers. The Kinnock modernisers were thoroughly parliamentarian and electoralist, and anything that went against this was seen as damaging the prospects of a Labour government. This explains their forthright opposition to all forms of militancy against the tax.

Trade union conservatism stems from the union structures themselves, as well as the people that populate them. Outside of periods of radicalisation, trade unions are essentially defensive organisations for the working class, wedded to a strategy of improving the lot of inevitably exploited workers. They are led by people on significantly higher wages than their members. The leaders see their role primarily as mediators and negotiators, which means that they view strikes and mass protests as weapons of last resort. Increasingly, trade union bureaucracies see strikes not as a means to inflict significant defeats on the bosses but as a method to bring them back to the negotiating table.

This attitude had been further entrenched by the anti-union laws imposed by the Conservatives during the 1980s, which forced the unions into incredibly narrow definitions of legality and specifically banned them from carrying out industrial action that was either political or seen as in solidarity with other workers. While trade unions themselves were still legal, the Tories had succeeded in making *effective* trade unionism illegal. This, coupled with the repeated significant industrial defeats meant that by the time the Poll Tax was implemented there was even less appetite for action from the trade union leaders than usual.

Since Labour is the political wing of British trade unionism, this general consciousness has seeped into the upper echelons of the party. Of course, over a hundred years Labour has evolved from simply being the representative of the trade unions in Parliament to a political party in its own right, with its own bureaucracies and ideological perspectives, but it still retains the general essence of the trade unions' role as moderators of capitalism's excesses who blanche at any radical action.

Although the boycotting of the campaign by the official labour organisations was a source of serious resentment and dispute at the time, it also meant that the Poll Tax movement was allowed to flourish and could not be co-opted. While socialists (more so than anarchists) often aim to include the official leaderships of Labour and the unions in campaigns in order to form a united front (or sometimes mainly to give legitimacy to an issue), such alliances will inevitably draw any radical initiative to the right. This is due to the inherently conservative nature of well-established bureaucracies that are wedded to the state or act as mediators of class struggle. Labour and the trade unions are both products and agencies of resistance to capitalism, but they seek to channel explosions of working-class anger in manageable directions which won't threaten the foundations of the system.[7]

The role of direct action in civil society

Debates on the legitimacy of extra-parliamentary, direct action campaigns have been happening for generations, turning on the question of what actions, if any, are acceptable beyond peaceful protest. These debates had been a central theme of the workers' movement since the 'physical force' arguments of the Chartists in the 1840s, and now the question of the nature of extra-parliamentary resistance went to the heart of the strategy of the Anti-Poll Tax movement.

This ethical debate can be summed up by the question Charles Frankel asked in the *New York Times* in 1964, in the context of the US Civil Rights movement: 'Is it right to break the law?' After rejecting the extreme view that civil disobedience and political law breaking is always wrong, he ponders whether it is permissible under a liberal democracy. Under such a system there are ostensibly institutions whereby grievances can be aired, either at the ballot box or through peaceful protests.

If a government has won an election without deploying nefarious means (beyond the usual hegemonic tools that capitalists use to maintain their rule, like the control of media and so on), then what right does a minority have to challenge that beyond registering a protest? Can it then be right for a dedicated minority to disrupt society for their own ends? 'This', Frankel wrote, 'is one of the standard arguments that is made, often quite sincerely, against the activities of people like supporters of the Congress of Racial Equality, who set about changing laws they find objectionable by dramatically breaking them. Such groups are often condemned for risking disorder and for spreading disrespect for the law when, so it is maintained, they could accomplish their goals a great deal more fairly and patriotically by staying within the law, and confining themselves to the courts and to methods of peaceful persuasion.'[8]

Frankel's argument is that there is a confusion between the ideals of democracy and its reality. After all, 'the police may be hostile, the courts biased, the elections rigged – and the legal remedies available to the individual may be unavailing against these evils'. In such a system, an embattled minority may be forced into actions beyond the traditional institutions or political procedures. The crucial factor is whether it is morally just to disobey the law.

Of course these moral arguments do not happen in a vacuum, removed from questions of power and class. The moral justification can be drawn either from liberal values of tolerance or from socialist values of class justice and a critique of the inequality of capitalism. It was right for Blacks in the United States to break the Jim Crow laws, but it would not be right for Neo-Nazis to break the law in order to impose a white supremacist regime.

The tension that exists within parliamentary liberal democracies is that between the official government, whose legitimacy rests on its electoral successes, and opponents of that government who might carry out disruptive extra-parliamentary actions designed to alter policy. In the face of popular struggles for social justice, bourgeois politicians and right-wing journalists argue vociferously for the primacy of Parliament as a decision-making body and for the *right* of politicians to rule. Their greatest fear is the 'mob', unruly, angry and threatening to property and personhood. Conversely, in the face of a left-wing government making inroads into capital and private property, there are a plethora of extra-parliamentary actions that the ruling class can carry out to effect policy (economic sabotage, currency speculation, media campaigns, 'dark money' destabilisation campaigns, etc). Everything depends on an ethical perspective over what is right and just – which side of the class struggle you are on.

The ideological reflex of arguing that parliamentary democracy is the only legitimate route for political change was clear in Thatcher's response to the rioting outside Hackney Town Hall. When asked about her views the next day, she remarked about the protests: 'I'm afraid it's one of a series which we know are being organised by Militant, as you know. And it is not the way to conduct affairs at all. In a democracy the way is to debate in Parliament, the legislation has been through Parliament, and anything that is intimidatory or violent is absolutely flatly contradictory to democracy. People can demonstrate, of course they can. They should do so peacefully ... they have got something to grouse about, but the way to do it is complain quietly.'⁹ This demand that opposition be limited to peaceful, 'quiet' complaints was precisely what revolutionaries and radicals rejected – even more so given how violent the British state had been in the 1980s, from the sinking of the Belgrano in the Falklands to the continued occupation of Northern Ireland, to police violence on picket lines and in the inner cities.

In this case, acts of civil disobedience – refusing to pay the Poll Tax, joining demonstrations where councils and courts were disrupted, and of course the riot in central London – were the actions of a sizeable minority who clearly understood the tax to be not only iniquitous but also a serious attack on their personal finances and therefore their well-being. The Tories believed they had a mandate for the Community Charge due to their victory in the 1987 general election. This argument clearly ignored the national question in Scotland and Wales, where the majority had rejected Conservative rule. Many saw this as an example of the tyranny of the majority. In such a case a concerted campaign by a minority can shift the entire argument and delegitimise a policy. This was very successful in the case of the Poll Tax, as by the end of the campaign close to 14 million people had either not paid or had underpaid – more than the 13.7 million that had voted Thatcher in for a third term.

The arguments around civil disobedience can also be understood in relation to concepts of legitimation and hegemony. The unpopularity of the tax to the point of mass non-payment represents a good example of what Jürgen Habermas describes as a *legitimation crisis*.¹⁰ In advanced capitalist economies the state intervenes directly in the economy, hence there is less of a direct class struggle because questions of surplus redistribution are decided politically. But the state requires legitimacy to act, and there are times when it can fail to secure that legitimacy and therefore loses the loyalty of the masses. Taxes are a crucial plank of any social contract between the government and its citizens (or subjects) – a redistribution of money to pay for spending that, ideally, should benefit the political community as defined by the nation. It is on this basis that governments secure the legitimacy of taxes. While individual tax dodging is relatively common (certainly among the rich), mass tax resistance is far rarer – the trigger in the case of the Poll Tax was a crisis of legitimation in the political regime. The gulf between the Conservatives' view of the legitimacy of the tax and the view of the general public was simply unbridgeable.

This general approach can also be seen in Stuart Hall's Gramscian conception of Thatcherism as a hegemonic ruling class project.[11] Thatcherism was successful in shifting the political terrain from the 1980s onwards, but no regime enjoys total ideological domination, even if the resistance to it is relatively weak and largely clandestine. Hegemony is a battleground, and establishing it requires a fight at every level – political, cultural and socio-economic. Thatcherism was contested at every turn during the 1980s. However, not until the Poll Tax did a truly mass opposition emerge to challenge the fundamental principles of the Thatcherite project.

Marx, writing in 1849, made a prescient point about the role of anti-tax protests throughout history, arguing that a crisis over taxes is usually a sign of a deeper social malaise: 'The refusal to pay taxes is merely a sign of the dissidence that exists between the Crown and the people, merely evidence that the conflict between the government and the people has reached a menacing degree of intensity. It is not the cause of the discord or the conflict, it is merely an expression of this fact. At the worst, it leads to the overthrow of the existing government, the existing political system. The foundations of society are not affected by this. In the present case, moreover, the refusal to pay taxes was a means of society's self-defence against a government which threatened its foundations.'[12]

It was in such a social context that the introduction of the Poll Tax acted as a detonator for an explosion of civil disobedience. The preceding decade of Thatcherism was the tinder. Both as an ideological challenge to municipal socialism and as a practical way of redistributing wealth from the poor to the rich, the Community Charge represented a New Right 'endgame' attack that had political, economic and social objectives.

It was at its heart a class struggle, but not one fought in the workplace; it was fought in the estates and in the council chambers. The government's failure to establish the legitimacy of the Poll Tax led to fractures in the Thatcherite hegemony. But, as we shall see, the protests failed to overthrow that hegemony in its entirety.

PART II

There were two important dimensions to the Anti-Poll Tax movement: it was both a struggle at the point of consumption and a struggle at the point of social reproduction. The issue of consumption relates to the battle over the social surplus in society, primarily people's wages and benefits. The question of how much money you have to live on is directly connected to the basic question of whether can you afford to eat, clothe yourself, pay for your housing, cover your bills and afford a degree of socialising. The high cost of the Poll Tax wasn't just egregious, it struck at the heart of this question of social reproduction. Ewan Gibbs draws a parallel between the Poll Tax years and the situation in cities like Detroit in the 1970s, when the class struggle was not limited to the factory floor but became a wider question of social life itself.[13] Social reproduction and consumption not only point to the issues at stake, but also to where resistance could be manifested.

However, struggles narrowly focused on consumption can often be ultimately self-limiting. In the case of the Poll Tax, the focus on resistance at the point of consumption meant that when the tax was defeated, consumers simply went back to their normal lives, eventually paying a different tax to the one that had been imposed upon them before. If you compare previous moments of crisis due to mass strike action – the General Strike of 1926, the miners' strike of 1974 and the Winter of Discontent in 1978 – they all led to a change of government at the next election. Why did the Anti-Poll Tax movement not either extend into a wider anti-Tory campaign or launch serious destabilising industrial action?

Militant's own strategy partly contributed to the limitations of what came next. While their single-minded focus on the non-payment strategy helped direct the movement and focus it on achieving its goal, that goal was ultimately limited. It meant that the campaign never unleashed the wider social forces that would have led to far more destabilisation and opened up the possibility of a seismic political shift. The lack of workers taking action throughout the economy ensured that the flows of power, profit and wealth that are the lifeblood of capitalism were never really threatened. The Anti-Poll Tax disruption – though widespread – never turned into a movement of rupture more generally.

Networks like 3D sought to develop 'a rounded political strategy that places non-payment within a framework of action within the unions and broader labour movement'.[14] They were explicitly critical of Militant's singular focus. But these networks were unable to shift the working class *as workers* into opposition. So, although it turned out that mass action by organised groups of workers in their workplaces was not necessary for beating the Community Charge, because the movement did not generalise forms of action that might have unleashed broader social forces in the workplace, it did not stem the overall long term decline of the British workers' movement or of the socialist left.

Socialists saw in the mass resistance the embryo of a future mass workers movement, spontaneously collectivist and radical. In Scotland, Militant attempted to carry the spirit and organising methods of the Anti-Poll Tax movement over into campaigns against water privatisation and domestic violence. While these campaigns did some important work, they turned out to be the last gasp of the movement, held together by people who had been radicalised by the fight against the Poll Tax, while most other activists returned to their ordinary lives. Again, this shows how a protest against taxation can become very radical very quickly, but also has its limitations.

Importantly, the Poll Tax struggle emerged at the end of a long period of political and industrial defeat for the working class. It was partly characterised therefore by its *defensive* character, as a desperate struggle to stop the seemingly unending onslaught of Thatcherite social engineering. While defensive struggles can give way to more offensive manoeuvres, this is far less common. This naturally placed obstacles in the way of the movement's ability to take more radical positions, and ultimately prevented it from evolving into a fight against the Major government. The key point here is that almost all of the struggles by the working class and the left under Thatcherism, certainly from 1982 onwards, were defensive. But there were also conscious efforts by the leadership of the trade unions and the labour movement to limit the resistance to Thatcherism and prevent a more radical fight that would threaten not only the government but the entire direction of British capitalism.

Was it even a social movement?

There is some disagreement over whether the fight to stop the Poll Tax can be classified as a social movement. It certainly had a lot of the features of such a movement: protests, meetings, cultural events, civil disobedience actions and a coherent political demand. It was also organised more along a network model than that of a centralised political party. Whether to categorise the campaign as a social movement or not is not a dry academic question. Addressing it can help illuminate our understanding of grassroots politics and its workings, and indicate to what degree cases of such politics amount to an organic mass movement. In his book *Social Movements in Britain*, Paul Byrne rejects the idea that the Anti-Poll Tax campaign was a social movement. He argues that it did not aim at broad social change based on certain values (as, for example, CND does as part of the wider 'peace movement'). Byrne's analysis is that it was a single-issue protest campaign focused on a particular goal, such that, once that goal was achieved, the campaign simply came to an end. He argues that the movement's failure to widen its demands into a systematic battle over cultural and political issues meant that it failed to transcend its role as a mere protest campaign: 'a social movement, because of its emphasis upon widespread beliefs and values, has *scope* and potential *durability* that a protest campaign does not'.[15]

There is an element of truth in this. The Anti-Poll Tax campaign was mobilised around a single issue, proven by the fact that when its demand was met the campaign ended. But we also have to consider the campaign in the context of the wider struggles of the 1980s. Even by Byrne's definition there was clearly a broader social movement against Thatcherism. It started in 1979 with a protest march in Brixton called by Lambeth Council, and went on to include mass strikes (by miners, steel workers and print workers) and protests, which saw huge solidarity networks being built as well as the aggregation of previously existing campaigns into an anti-Thatcher, anti-Tory struggle, as for instance with the feminists and peace campaigners at Greenham Common. To a large degree, the inner city riots of 1981 were also an example of resistance to Thatcher's policing and managed urban decline policies. The left in the 1980s was thus defined by a wider social movement based on political, cultural and social values *contra* Thatcher – and the Anti-Poll Tax campaign was only the latest expression of that struggle.

The question of continuity in radical politics – the way that people can become veterans of struggles, bringing resources and organising abilities to new movements from previous ones – is important. Indeed, any resistance movement will 'require the successful connection of current struggles with previous ones'.[16] A number of the APTUs were established from already existing networks of activists who had come together during the various struggles prior to the campaign, most notably the solidarity groups with the miners. In Bridgwater the miners' solidarity campaign simply evolved into an APTU. Some activists who had been fighting the Tories for years saw the fight against the Poll Tax as merely the latest round in that struggle. Jeff Goulding was a typical example: 'When the Poll Tax was introduced, I can honestly say I was primarily motivated by the opportunity to take on Thatcher *again*, and maybe inflict a fatal blow to the Tories. It was not until later that I reflected on the fact that the Poll Tax was functionally unjust and would inflict misery on millions of people.'[17]

And it wasn't just the organisers, it was a lot of the people on the protests. A useful example was the Hackney protests in March 1990. The organisers had made it clear that there was a general history of police violence in the borough, including deaths in custody, which had got worse under Thatcher. The general sense of a community under siege by a racist and violent police force contributed to the violent scenes outside the town hall when the Poll Tax was set. Some of the organisers were already hardened campaigners who could mobilise people from previous movements around specific issues.

PART III

New vs old, or the death of the working class?

Within social movement theory there is a school of thought that posits a distinction between old and new social movements. For a movement to be considered 'old', sociologists characterise it as one based on economic material conditions – essentially identifying them as class-based struggles usually involving traditional organisations, for instance trade unions. A social movement earns the label 'new' if it is concentrated more on 'issues', for instance nuclear weapons, environmentalism, anti-racism, etc.[18] This shift represents a shift from working-class social movements to middle-class ones. From this perspective, the old left was corporatist and social democratic whereas the new left is non-hierarchical and focused on symbolic actions around single issues.[19]

Alongside these academic debates there was a growing body of thought in the 1980s that saw shifts in politics internationally as well as in Britain away from straightforwardly industrial working-class struggles (similar to the concept of the old social movements), and a decline in previous forms of class consciousness. This 'retreat from class', as Ellen Woods described it, has both hard and soft readings, from the emphasis on new forms of left populism in Chantal Mouffe and Ernesto Laclau's *Hegemony and Socialist Strategy* (1985) or André Gorz's *Farewell to the Working Class* (1982), to *Marxism Today*'s political trajectory and Eric Hobsbawm's *The Forward March of Labour Halted?* (1982).

There was a general theme: left-wing politics was no longer a matter of powerful trade unions squaring off against the bosses and the Tories, as had been the case for the last 100 years. Things had shifted. It was now (working) people engaging in new struggles from below, independently of their established organisations, that would characterise social struggles going forward. Working-class people were less likely to struggle as workers and instead fight as consumers. Resistance was less likely to happen at the point of production and more likely to occur at the point of social circulation. Essentially, the purely proletarian socialist working-class movement was finished, if it had ever really existed, having been replaced by broader populist left alliances or specifically non-working-class political forces. Socialism was replaced with populism or by broad alliances of 'the left'.

In this sense, arguably, the Anti-Poll Tax movement could be understood through the prism of a retreat from (or an alternative to) the traditional organised working-class movement, as an individualist response in which militancy stemmed from a desire for 'a private niche protecting one's personal life against all pressures and external social obligations'.[20] It had the appearance of a mass working-class revolt with nascent socialist elements in it, but this was an illusion. It was a turning point between the battles of the miners' strike and Wapping and the new forms of radicalism of the 1990s, such as the campaign against the Criminal Justice Bill, and Reclaim the Streets.

But Marxist terms of analysis can still explain how the movement emerged and its relationship to the state and to the existing labour movement. The political trajectory of the Labour and union leaders also had an impact on the forces involved in the struggle. The retreat from class could clearly be seen in Labour: Kinnockism was the gateway drug for Blairism, which culminated in the 'we are all middle class now' ethos of aspirational Cool Britannia. One crucial conveyor belt for this ideological shift was the Communist Party of Great Britain. Ironically, their particular evolution during the course of the 1980s (see Chapter 3) should have allowed them a greater orientation to this mass movement. Martin Jacques, the editor of *Marxism Today*, had written as far back as 1979 that it was important not to 'underestimate the extent of the crisis and the range of issues around which popular support can be mobilised'.[21] The focus on purely 'economistic' trade union struggles was already fading, and a decisive political shift towards new social movements had already taken root in the party. But, Icarus like, they flew too close to the sun. Their political strategy had abandoned the working class as an agent for revolutionary social change. The CPGB's appeal for the Anti-Poll Tax movement to be more like Comic Relief was indicative of a political force that no longer saw the possibilities embedded within contemporary struggles for radical social change. Instead it was a plea for better, broader *institutional* alliances of the great and the good. More comedians, more bishops, less strikes, less socialism.

The lack of involvement from the official labour movement had an impact on The Demo in particular. While Militant had wanted it to be a labour movement protest, replete with trade union banners and possibly a colliery marching band, what they got was a tumultuous popular protest of the poor marching alongside the radical left. It was increasingly becoming the case that the radicalism of a particular political action was in inverse proportion to the level of TUC and 'official labour movement' involvement.

Likewise the defeats of the local government left and the most militant trade unions meant that any coherent resistance from these forces was by 1989 highly unlikely. The Anti-Poll Tax movement had to go it alone, without the structural or organisational power of the workers' movement. This partly explains why – despite its victory – the movement had no lasting repercussions in terms of a revival of the Labour left or the trade unions. They were inoculated from it by prior defeats. This is not to say that individuals from the unions were not involved, but they could not pull their organisations with them nor could they instil the spirit of resistance back into the unions afterwards.

A recent book by Joshua Glover provides a framework to look at the historical place of the movement in a shifting political landscape of resistance. In *Riot. Strike. Riot.*, Glover identifies three distinct periods of working-class struggle. The first is the period of explosive early capitalist riots, usually over the price of goods like food, up until the turn of the nineteenth century. This is followed by the period of strikes, from 1842 onwards, where trade unions became formal institutions and leveraged industrial action over the price of labour. The third period is the current phase of riots – inner-city clashes with the police, often racial in dimension, a form of conflict that becomes more common as the power of the organised working class is chipped away at by neoliberalism.

Although Glover does not include the Poll Tax campaign, the clashes with police outside council chambers and the riot in Trafalgar Square would certainly fit his description of a trade union and labour movement in retreat while the working class bursts forth to fight over the question of the price of market goods – in this case the unaffordable good being the Community Charge. The flat-rate payment people had to make for local services was simply priced too high in the marketplace. And much like the grain riots of yesteryear, the new tumult was the result of an explosive uprising of proletarians and an urban underclass who simply could not afford to pay.[22] There is one crucial difference however; for Glover the new riots were also racialised, based as they were in inner-city communities. The Trafalgar Square riot was not racialised in the same way as those at Broadwater Farm or Brixton had been previously. This was also one reason why it was harder for the political establishment to dismiss it using racist framing.

The failure to build the movement into a campaign against water privatisation through the non-payment strategy also provides an interesting insight into the question of how political consciousness and resistance are formed. Gorz's argument would be that the campaign against water privatisation failed because – unlike the Community Charge – the privatisation was not directed at individuals. The immediate impact of the Poll Tax on people's bank accounts and quality of life was obvious. And while the left always made the argument that privatisation would ultimately increase the cost of something (train tickets, water bills, etc.), in Britain in the 1980s this was never enough to spark a mass movement of resistance.

So, was it an old or new social movement? Paul Bagguley makes a compelling case that the Anti-Poll Tax movement was an eclectic blend of both.[23] After all, it clearly identified with old social movement traditions (class, socialism, etc.) while also organising much more in the manner of a new social movement, with the APTUs as nodes in a network spanning the length of the British Isles. While material issues were central (poverty, unaffordable taxes), and therefore the question of class was a predominant one, it was a movement largely outside of the traditional institutions of the working class. The trade unions and Labour Party vacated the field of struggle early on. Of course, the contradiction is that Militant and other socialists involved in the campaign were still based in the labour movement more generally – but they had to establish a campaigning organisation to overcome the inertia or outright political hostility from the official labour leaders. The fight against the Poll Tax even deployed symbolic actions straight out of the CND playbook in the 1950s, for instance the Committee of 100.

And when historians like Ewan Gibbs draw historical parallels between struggles such as the 1915 Glasgow rent strikes with the Anti-Poll Tax movement, or when Tommy Sheridan highlights the historical continuities with the radicalism of working-class communities, we can see that class and traditional left politics mattered to this struggle. We will explore this further in the next section.

From a Marxist analytical point of view though, the categories of old and new social movements have only limited utility. The danger of such an academic bifurcation is that it comes across as ahistorical and, as John Krinsky argues, overstates the novelty of the supposed 'new', preferring 'generalisations about culture and cultural change to more grounded criticisms of socio-cultural dynamics'.[24] Indeed all the mainstream academic accounts of social movements only really look at particular aspects of them (their resources, their organising models, etc.) and often sidestep the bigger questions of 'power, the economy and the state'.[25]

PART IV

The principal contribution of Marxist theory to any study of a social movement or formation is to highlight the role of class – how classes are formed and the antagonistic relationship between them – which is an essential aspect of the coming into being of class consciousness. While on the surface the Poll Tax struggle was over who would shoulder the burden of the cost of local government funding, this conflict has to be seen in the context of the great battles of the 1980s, which was an intense period of class war in which the old social democratic consensus was ripped up to be replaced with a new economic regime that would make

Britain more profitable for its capitalist class. The goal of the Thatcherite project was both to reintroduce structural mass unemployment to break the power of trade unionism, and to privatise state industries to allow the more competitive and 'disciplined' free market to gorge itself on those parts of the economy to which it had hitherto been denied access. The idea, in other words, was to restore British capitalism to full health while banishing the collectivist sickness. The combined effect of these policies was to enlarge the poorer and more deprived sections of the working class. Of course, Thatcher's project was also intended to drive inflation out of the economy, something that it had manifestly failed to achieve by the time of the Poll Tax. This led to an economic squeeze for those in work as well as those unemployed – prices were going up faster than wages were.

As such, both the philosophy behind the Community Charge and the resistance to it can be seen as condensed acts of class politics, of class warfare. The class dynamics found expression in the way that the opposition to the Poll Tax was formulated, explained and coordinated by the movement. This was a struggle replete with class arguments and antagonisms against the rich and against the Conservatives. The populist rhetoric of Thatcherism was fatally undermined by the Community Charge. It was not seen as an equality of opportunity – part of the rising tide that would lift all boats – but understood as an unfair, class-based attack on the poor by an out of touch government. Thatcherism had over-reached and in doing so had begun to eat itself.

Those who could not afford to pay the tax made up the majority of non-payers: pensioners, single mothers, ethnic minorities, the disabled, the unemployed and underemployed – all those who had suffered most under the rapacious capitalist and free market ideology. Alongside these people in the core of refuseniks stood class-conscious workers and activists who refused to pay on principle. The Community Charge went beyond cuts to local services or anti-trade union legislation, and even beyond the attacks on the miners in 1984–5. This was the first time that the entire population had been targeted as individuals. Thatcherism had come to everyone's house. Here was a chance for mass opposition to a 'flagship policy' and people seized upon it. The millions of poor made poorer by New Right ideology had a chance for revenge, for mass opposition. The class dimension here is inescapable.

The important role that urban centres played in the campaign also points to an alliance of the working-class and the urban poor as the critical mass of the campaign. The huge non-payment campaigns in Glasgow, Leeds, Sheffield, Bristol, Manchester and London, usually either led or at least influenced by the socialist left, were decisive in providing the millions of non-payers that helped defeat the Community Charge.

However the mass non-payment campaign also reached into the middle classes and, as we have seen, some of the most vociferous protests came from parts of southern England that were considered far more petty bourgeois than proletarian. It is clear that any mass movement such as the Anti-Poll Tax campaign would involve wider social forces beyond the working class. While the movement was inevitably very strong in the metropolitan urban centres, active APTUs could also be found in many towns and smaller cities where the far left were much weaker and the class composition was not as straightforwardly proletarian.

It would be an error to reduce the struggle against the Poll Tax to a simplistic labour/capital struggle perspective that did not also take into account gender and ethnicity. Whether the mother struggling to balance household bills with feeding and clothing her family, or the woman in waged labour who becomes financially responsible for her male partner, the Community Charge was a direct attack on the living standards of many millions of women. Ethnic minority families – statistically likely to be larger than white British families – also had to shoulder a much bigger financial burden if they had adult children living at home. This also raised questions of youth social oppression; in a time before the minimum wage, a 19 year old could be working for very little money and yet have to pay as much tax as their father, who would often be on a much higher wage.

The important analytical point in any account of a struggle such as that of the Poll Tax is to understand the role of class not as a distinct category but as a social relation, as a question of how people struggle as they move through their own contradictions. Working-class-based resistance usually starts from capital's impact on the individual: a wage cut, longer working hours, job losses and potential impoverishment. Only very rarely does the working class struggle first and foremost for political goals – but when it does so, this indicates the crystallisation of a socialist class consciousness on a very high level. As the historian E.P. Thompson argued: 'To put it bluntly: classes do not exist as separate entities, look around, find an enemy class, and then start to struggle. On the contrary, people find themselves in a society structured in determined ways (crucially, but not exclusively, in productive relations), they experience exploitation (or the need to maintain power over those whom they exploit), they identify points of antagonistic interest, they commence to struggle around these issues and in the process of struggling they discover themselves as classes, they come to know this discovery as class-consciousness. Class and class-consciousness are always the last, not the first, stage in the real historical process.'[26]

Thompson's conception of class is useful here in trying to understand a broad movement which included some of the poorest people in society alongside sections of organised workers and even parts of the middle classes. Because class is a social relation, it is largely only identifiable when the relationship becomes clearly antagonistic. Thompson's argument against mainstream historians who would go down into the 'engine-room' of history to look around and 'tell us that nowhere at all have they been able to locate and classify a class' was that they were being too scholastic. They could not see the wood for the trees. 'They can only find a multitude of people with different occupations, incomes, status hierarchies, and the rest. Of course they are right, for class is not this or that part of the machine, but the way the machine works once it is set in motion – not this interest and that interest but the friction of interests – the movement itself, the heat, the thundering noise.'[27]

For many activists the fight against the Poll Tax connected to historic working-class struggles such as the 1915 rent strike in Glasgow or the Upper Clyde Shipyard work-in of 1971–72.[28] As the campaign developed, references to historical events became more commonplace, giving a sense of moral legitimacy to the fight to break the tax. There was the 1381 Peasants' Revolt of course, but the Glasgow rent strikes and the postwar industrial disputes on the Clyde had particular resonance for the Scottish, while the Chartist movement was also a reference point for the campaign in England and Wales, especially in relation to the size and geographical spread of local protests. Even the mass protests against the Corn Laws were occasionally referenced, usually by Conservatives to refer to the last time widespread civil disturbances had caused a historic crisis for the government. The riot in Trafalgar Square had living connectivity to the 1981 summer riots in Brixton, Toxteth and elsewhere, to the 1985 Brixton and Broadwater Estate riots, and further back to the Gordon Riots of 1780.

For the historic working-class movement there was no clear division between industrial and community struggles – the men and women

who lived in places like Govan had also worked in the nearby industries, and the difference between a rent strike and a workplace strike was
only a matter of perspective, a question of the short walk between the
factory and the housing estate. Trade union activists who were leaders
at work would often be found leading tenant associations or community
organisations – they knew the value of collective organisation and solidarity when it came to winning concessions from the powerful. Tommy
Sheridan and Militant drew inspiration from these struggles, rein-
forcing the sense of historical resistance: 'Again and again during our
campaign we returned to the Clydeside rent strikes. Every poinding we
stopped was inspired by those wartime women. They would hang out the
windows, banging their pots and pan when they saw the sheriffs coming.
Our eyes and ears had proved just as keen. We had succeeded in reviving
the tradition of struggle.'[29]

In part then, the battle of Militant and the rest of the Labour socialist
left against the Kinnock leadership was one of competing claims to historical tradition and justification. When Kinnock argued that the party
could be one of either protest or power, he was urging members to make
a decision: choose the party of Ramsay MacDonald and Hugh Gaitskell
or the party of direct action advocated by James Maxton, Tony Benn and
other renegades of the Labour left. These competing views of Labour –
as a purely electoralist party that had to accommodate for votes or as a
campaigning social movement – were played out in the battle over the
Poll Tax.

Conclusions

What strategic considerations can we draw from radical social movements
which aim to disrupt and destabilise governments, as opposed to those
that want to apply pressure for more moderate ends? There are three
that we can develop from the experience of the Anti-Poll-Tax campaign,
concerning points of resistance, the crystallisation of antagonisms, and
the importance of new organisations.

Points of resistance

A model of organising based on that of the ABAPTF was adopted
again for the Stop the War Coalition (StWC) established in 2001. Led
by a national executive and with a delegate conference that adopted
motions, the local groups remained relatively autonomous, though they

had far more uniform branding and materials than the Anti-Poll Tax movement did. However, there were inevitably differences in how the two movements operated, given the nature of the goals of each. In the Poll Tax campaign, there was one massive demonstration that turned into a riot alongside some other protests, though demonstrations were never the backbone of the campaign. The fight to stop the Community Charge happened on the doorsteps of homes up and down the country, confronting and chasing away bailiffs and sheriffs. It happened in courts in every major city and town as people were summonsed before the magistrates. It also happened in local protests outside council chambers, however little impact they had on the decisions of the councillors inside.

The StWC relied more on protest marches as the key plank of their campaign. From the perspective that Danny Burns laid out in 1992, the StWC was a movement of protest, not one of *resistance*. Here we can begin to develop a theory around resistance as opposed to mere protest. Resistance must involve acts which frustrate the effective workings of social or political mechanisms. In the words of student activist Mario Savio during the Berkeley Free Speech Movement in the 1960s: 'You've got to put your bodies upon the gears and upon the wheels ... upon the levers, upon all the apparatus, and you've got to make it stop. And you've got to indicate to the people who run it, to the people who own it, that unless you're free, the machine will be prevented from working at all!'

The question then becomes one of disruption, and that almost always involves some element of law-breaking even if it is civil law and not criminal. When the laws are designed to ensure the effective operation of capitalism as a socio-economic system, then a clash between the popular aspirations of a resistance movement – whether attempting to prevent something from occurring or putting forward a positive agenda for change – and the legal apparatus of society is inevitable.

Resistance requires bodies to be pressed against the gears and the wheels, it means actions to sabotage or break a system or a structure. This was possible with the Poll Tax because it affected everyone in the country; millions of people could be drawn into a fight in which they had a personal stake. For the StWC, however, the war was in Afghanistan and Iraq. Adopting similar tactics to the Anti-Poll Tax movement would have required taking more direct action, such as trying to prevent the military machine from mobilising. There was one notable instance of industrial resistance, when train drivers in Motherwell refused to move a train full of munitions, but – much like the Greenwich NALGO action against the tax – this was an isolated action by a handful of workers.

Away from the stifling timidity of the unions, the social composition of the Anti-Poll Tax movement allowed for a plethora of points of resistance. Traditionally, the inclusion of poorer people in social or protest movements has been harder to achieve or sustain; they are often harder to reach, may have less traditional collective organisation, and may be more suspicious of 'political agitators' than are those sections of the working or middle classes who are involved in civil society through pressure groups or trade unions. But because the Community Charge affected every resident in every region, it allowed a variety of decentralised actions to occur. As described in this book, the ABAPTF provided some national leadership, but essentially the movement was made up of largely autonomous local groups established in towns and cities (even occasionally villages) across Britain. This created opportunities for resistance that many people could be involved in regardless of wealth or social capital.

Crystallisation of antagonisms

While points of resistance refer to specific oppositional acts, to the *physicality* of opposition, the next level of analysis points to how the generalised opposition crystallises at different levels of society and politics, causing ruptures in the political hegemony of the ruling class.

In *The German Ideology* Marx and Engels wrote, 'the ideas of the ruling class are in every epoch the ruling ideas, i.e. the class which is the ruling material force of society, is at the same time its ruling intellectual force'.[30] These hegemonic ideas are produced and reinforced by the smooth running of the economy, politics and society. A struggle from below can disrupt this smooth operation of the hegemony machine.

Alongside the points of resistance in the implementation of the Community Charge, there were several crises within the hegemony of the Conservative Party. The first one was the broadest: millions of people not paying their tax represented a decisive break with the social contract which exists between government and citizens. A certain amount of tax avoidance is common in society, usually among middle-class entrepreneurs who don't fill out their tax returns properly, and most notoriously among the super-rich who evade taxes altogether by keeping their money offshore, or through complicated accounting measures that obscure the true measure of their wealth. It is the working classes, paying through their wages, that have to pay tax on a regular and consistent basis. The mass non-payment of taxes was thus a huge political and psychological shift for millions of people, whether they opposed the government unwillingly simply because they could not afford to pay the tax, or chose to fight because they were ideologically motivated against it.

The next dimension was the declining support for the tax and for Thatcher herself. While her personal approval ratings had risen and fallen throughout the 1980s, the manner in which the dislike of both her and of her flagship policy coincided proved to be politically deadly. This only added to the general feeling among Tory MPs that something had to change, and led to disastrous by-elections in which safe Conservative seats fell to opposition parties who made the Poll Tax the central issue of their campaigns. These by-election results were traumatic ruptures within the political regime, each one a blow to the confidence of the governing class.

Building better tools

Clearly the existing politics of the workers' movement and Labourism were utterly insufficient to beat the Poll Tax. This manifested in the manner in which the mass organisations of the labour movement ultimately had to be bypassed in order to leverage social forces into a direct action campaign. While raising the argument within these mass organisations is an important component of any radical campaign, ultimately if the tools to hand are inadequate then new tools must be created. The formation of the APTUs and the various regional or national federations that organised the campaign, while they were greeted with hostility by the press and the labour movement, were an irreplaceable tool to create and sustain the movement.

But it isn't just new organisations that are necessary at different stages of any particular struggle. In the case of the Poll Tax, the existence of socialist organisations such as Militant and of established networks of anarchist activists was essential to giving the mass movement the organisational capacity to marshal broad forces and generalise lessons within the resistance. Leaving such tasks to inchoate 'spontaneous' forces can result in political unevenness or practical confusion in the face of a political enemy that is (usually) well organised and centralised. It is worth adding that whenever a meeting, a strike or a protest is described as having been 'spontaneous', it simply means that the history books do not record who spoke up first, or who was the first to walk out. So-called spontaneous action is often initiated by people with a critical consciousness that puts them in a position of momentary leadership. So it was with the APTUs set up across the country, many of them initially called by socialists or anarchists or other campaigners who had already been fighting Thatcherism for years. What the Anti-Poll Tax movement did, and did well, was create an organisation that channelled those forces in such a way as to deliver a death blow to a flagship government policy.

Conclusion:
A System Shaken or Broken?

The Community Charge became synonymous with catastrophic government failure. It was a misconceived, vicious piece of class legislation. In the febrile climate of late 1980s Britain, such a calculated and ostentatious attack on so many people was bound to galvanise opposition. The government's failure to foresee that was a supreme moment of hubris.

But even on its own terms the Community Charge did not succeed. The argument that the poor could be persuaded to vote Tory by slapping them with huge bills didn't work, in large part because the poor didn't really vote. The Tory view that the middle and upper classes were being made to pay more because the Labour-supporting poor outvoted them was empirically untrue.[1] Instead of blaming local Labour councils, people largely blamed the government for the excessively high charges. The tax also failed to discipline local councils financially. The Tories had to impose their own caps to keep the Poll Tax bills low, which defeated the entire point of the financial reforms. And, as Lawson and others had predicted, it ended up costing central government more money than it saved.

Behind all the grand philosophies and pronouncements on the justice of the Poll Tax, it was clear that the overriding priority was to further undermine local government autonomy. Even John Gibson, who was generally sympathetic to the Thatcherite reforms of local government in the 1980s, concluded that 'throughout, Parliament and the British public were expected to believe in the strength of the Government's commitment to their theory of greater local accountability through the poll tax. Greater local accountability has turned out to be only a "cover story" – a cover for the only real objective: to cut expenditure.'[2]

The defeat of the Poll Tax, however, was not the end of the story. There were several fall-outs from the campaign that made their mark on British politics. The Tories got a very bloody nose. Their ideology, when it was tested on everyone equally and not just trade unionists or the public sector, proved deeply unpopular. The New Right theory simply did not match up with the lived experience of millions of people. Even paying a small amount in local tax was simply impossible for some people, particularly those who had suffered most after a decade of Thatcherite economics had devastated their communities.

As we have seen, there has been much debate about the causes of Thatcher's resignation. Many on the left like to pin it all on the Poll Tax movement, others point primarily to the divisions over Europe. Certainly, alongside the Poll Tax, there was an accumulation of contradictions towards the end of her premiership: the rift in her party over Europe, the manoeuvres by the 'wet' opponents against 'hard' Thatcherism (people like Heseltine), the loss of all her allies in Cabinet, and a general sense that she was losing her touch as the Iron Lady, that the 'economic miracle' she had presided over was drawing to an end.

These contradictions could have continued until 1992 – Thatcher could have led the Tories into the next general election – but the fear in the bellies of Conservative MPs was that the Poll Tax issue would cost them their seats. It was clear that the Community Charge either needed to be scrapped or be subject to even more fundamental reform, neither of which Thatcher was willing to countenance. It was the self-interest of parliamentarians that provided the ignition for the funeral pyre, the fire that ended Thatcher's time as Prime Minister. As such, we can conclude that the movement against the Community Charge was a significant contributing factor in her downfall.

The Tories ultimately survived for another five years because they replaced Thatcher, abolished the Poll Tax, and distanced themselves, at least rhetorically, from the worst excesses of Thatcherism. They succeeded in doubling down on their strengths and hammering Labour on its perceived weaknesses. By contrast Labour still looked like it was embroiled in a civil war, and Kinnock ran a half-hearted campaign in 1992 which pleased no one enough to win government. Labour's official position of opposition to non-payment and its hard-nosed pragmatism around imprisoning Poll Tax resisters meant that the anger and energy whipped up by the movement simply could not be transferred to the Labour Party in any organised or consistent way.

Labour's position was also predicated on the assumption that they would win in 1992 and so be able to abolish the tax. But what if the movement had not existed and Labour had still lost? If there had been no movement against the tax, making the case for non-payment and supporting refuseniks, then it is possible that it would have survived, with some modifications. Given enough time and space the Tories could have expanded the rebate system to encompass more of those simply unable to pay, dividing those not paying on principle from those not paying due to poverty. Perhaps we would still have a modified form of the Poll Tax today.

Although the subsequent years of neoliberalism under Tony Blair's New Labour had profoundly negative impacts on a range of people and public services, arguably it could have been far worse if the Poll Tax had remained in place. It was both the culmination of the Thatcherite agenda but also the thin end of the wedge for a whole new round of attacks and 'reforms' that would have fundamentally shifted Britain even further to the right.

It was the concept of a moral economy that allowed the far left and anarchists to assume the leadership of a mass movement. Once you establish that a tax is manifestly unjust, that it is ethically and morally *wrong*, then those who can both explain why it is happening and offer up resistance to it will do far better than politicians who wring their hands over it and make speeches against it, but ultimately accept it. The Poll Tax made the Labour leadership look cynical, as it became clear they were grasping after power and had no serious answer to the moral question of non-payment.

Since Labour had abrogated responsibility, who could claim the honours for the defeat of the Poll Tax? Naturally, Militant argued that it was their strategy that had led to victory. They were the largest organisation on the ground arguing for and pursuing the mass non-payment campaign. It was Militant organisers and members who provided the spinal column for the movement and staffed the HQ of the Federation, and they had an already existing network of people who were totally dedicated to the campaign. Other socialist groups either did not have the same resources or had a different strategy that proved to be a dead end.

The anarchists, for their part, sought to portray the campaign as a movement driven essentially (though perhaps unconsciously) by their principles of radical individual autonomy: it avoided the hierarchical bureaucracy of the trade unions and the Labour Party, it pursued independent working-class action, separate from the tired old-left organisations that had so singularly failed to halt Thatcherism, and it generated a full-scale riot where people confronted the state in a gratifying explosion of resistance. That riot was also different to the previous ones in Tottenham, Brixton and Toxteth. They were riots against the police, and against a general sense of urban decline – the riot of 31 March

1990 took place in central London, was huge, and was aimed directly at the heart of a government policy.

But the riot on its own did not stop the Community Charge. In the end the sheer numbers of non-payers, the overwhelmed bureaucracy, the chaos in the councils and the backlogs in the courts were what killed the tax. It was the actions of millions of people across the country, a combination of can't pay and won't pay, of people who had no financial means to pay the tax and those who were bitterly opposed to it, morally and politically. It was their intransigence that won. Militant gave the clearest singular message on non-payment, but in doing so the campaign was not broadened out into a movement against the Tories more generally. Its inability to really impact on and shift the trade unions or to develop into a wider social movement meant that when the tax was gone, so was the movement.

There are those who still believe that the principle behind the tax is sound. The Adam Smith Institute maintained even 20 years later that the concept of the Community Charge was perfectly workable, it was just the implementation of it that led to disaster. There might be some truth in the claim that the twin-track approach of phasing the tax in over time alongside more generous welfare payments (the original proposal from Douglas Mason) would have been more effective, but there are doubts as to whether the tax was sustainable in the long term. The growing numbers of people in prison, and of those not paying the full amount, seemed to indicate a more general crisis for the tax – simply that it was unaffordable for the very people who had already suffered most under Thatcherism. This might have resulted in voters punishing high-spending councillors at local elections, but that assumes that people would have eventually blamed Labour councils and not the Tories for the tax. Its failure is also rooted in the Conservative canard that local councils were profligate and wasteful, and that bills could be reduced without a huge impact on local services – in practice not a sustainable argument.

How did the events of the Poll Tax years change Britain? For one thing, they delivered a serious blow to attempts by the New Right to advance their policies in new directions. If the principle of the Poll Tax had survived then it might very well have made the idea of flat taxes in general more palatable. The psychological shift involved in seeing your local council payments not as a tax but as a 'charge' for services could well have gone some way towards gradually introducing such a principle into healthcare as well.

While the crisis significantly contributed to the downfall of Thatcher and thus, paradoxically, helped the Tories recover in time to win the 1992 general election, Labour doubled down on its purge of left-wingers, including precipitating a formal split with Militant. Kinnock's abdication of leadership over the Poll Tax campaign, and the party's subsequent defeat at the 1992 election, paved the way for the rise of Blairism, a rightward turn that was born out of defeats and demoralisation.[3] In large part, the continued advance of neoliberalism was due to Labour's own evolution into a social liberal party under Blair and the continuation of a variant of the same Thatcherite policies. No alternative political force in Britain emerged out of the struggles against Thatcherism that could either defend social democracy or advance a more radical socialist cause. The closest was the political evolution of the SNP and the temporary left turn of the Liberal Democrats under Charles Kennedy until 2006.

Since the Poll Tax was designed to alleviate Conservative electoral problems in Scotland, it was ironic that it did precisely the opposite, helping to accelerate the historic decline of the Conservative Party there. It opened the door for the left turn of the SNP and its eventual breakthrough a few years later as more Scots looked towards independence as a serious prospect.[4] Labour took a turn towards Scottish devolution under Kinnock, something that was later enacted under Blair. The Poll Tax was crucial in further fermenting a sense of national antagonism against Westminster and Tory domination from 'the south'. The later near-hegemony of the SNP in Scottish politics can be traced back to the events of the late 1980s.

The legacy of the Anti-Poll Tax campaign also had an impact on the far left. Scottish Militant Labour fused with other socialist groups to form the Scottish Socialist Alliance before launching as the Scottish Socialist Party. The SSP was briefly a leading party of the European left until it imploded in 2006 after an acrimonious dispute among the leadership. In 2003 it had six Members of the Scottish Parliament, many of them Poll Tax campaign veterans, including Sheridan. The party successfully brought a private member's bill to abolish poindings and warrant sales, a legacy of the hatred in working-class communities for the sheriffs during the fight against the Community Charge.

The Poll Tax events started a debate in Militant in England and Wales over whether 'entryism' in relation to the Labour Party was still a worthwhile strategy. Labour's defeat in 1992 and the vibrancy of the Poll Tax movement surely indicated that there was space for a new left party, one that was more radical than Labour and would advocate for the kind of 'old Labour' politics that Kinnock and his colleagues had abandoned. Others rejected this outlook, claiming that the stranglehold of the right was only temporary and that the working class only had one party – Labour. Every other attempt to launch an alternative had failed and would always fail. Thus a huge factional fight began between the majority who favoured leaving, centred around Peter Taaffe, and a minority who gathered around the group's historic leader, Ted Grant. Taaffe won, splitting Militant and leading the majority out of the organisation to form Militant Labour, before finally declaring themselves the Socialist Party in 1997.

The replacement policy, the Council Tax, was politically palatable enough not to generate any organised opposition, but it was also a regressive tax not based on ability to pay. The only concession was the property bands, based on formulas from 1992 and never re-evaluated since. The replacement never inspired protests in the same way that the Community Charge had done, but it was still iniquitous, as someone living in a one-bedroom flat in the Barbican would pay more than the Heseltine family living in their luxurious four-bedroom house in Belgravia.

Initially the poorest did not have to pay the new tax due to the Council Tax Benefit welfare scheme, but in 2013 the coalition government altered the legislation to allow councils to charge the poorest 20 per cent of the total bill. Overnight they reintroduced an element of the Poll Tax that had sparked so many protests the first time around. This time though, the changes slipped through without anyone taking much notice. A year later, three quarters of English councils were charging those on benefits. It worked out on average at £2.75 a week, but for someone on £71 a week benefits, that meant a 5 per cent cut in living standards.[5] This had a huge impact on debt levels. In 2017 Alan Murdie wrote an extensive article in *The Big Issue* about the growing numbers of people unable to pay their Council Tax. Money owed to local government surpassed credit card debt in 2014, and 3 million people were issued with liability orders in 2017.[6] Local authorities grappling with huge budget cuts pursued the poorest even more rigorously to boost their revenue streams, leading to what Citizens Advice described as a 'Council Tax debt epidemic' in 2019.[7]

The impact of the Community Charge on Labour in local government cannot be underestimated. In particular it marked a decisive shift in the attitude of Labour councillors. The experience of implementing the Poll Tax in the face of mass opposition led a new generation of

Labour councillors to see themselves as hard-nosed managers of local government who had to obey the law no matter what. Labour councillors had implemented cuts before, but this was a situation in which they were imprisoning people in order to break the back of a progressive movement. This marked a turning point where the entire political culture of Labour councillors shifted significantly to the right.

The story of the Anti-Poll Tax campaign is rich with historical lessons about how a government policy which impacts on so many people can be opposed by systemically building a campaign of resistance. The lessons include targeting the weakest points of the policy in relation to its social consequences, the importance of making a clear class argument, the need to unite a broad range of people, and the symbolic significance of being prepared to risk imprisonment if necessary. This combination of factors produced the powerful movement against the Poll Tax that struck deep into the heart of British society. When the masses lose their fear, when the police, the prisons, the judges and threats of poverty are no longer enough to keep the people in line, then petitions can lead to protests that can cause political explosions. The power of a mass movement dedicated to victory can melt even an Iron Lady.

Notes

Introduction

1. Ivor Crewe and Anthony King, *The Blunders of our Governments* (London: Oneworld, 2013), Chapter 4, p. 41.
2. 'Esther McVey Admits Universal Credit Claimants "will be worse off" in Car Crash Interview as Tory Fury Mounts', *Daily Mirror*, 12 October 2018.
3. See https://www.bbc.co.uk/news/uk-scotland-26013711.
4. 'Speed Trap Alarms for Drivers to be Banned', *Independent*, 17 September 2000.

Chapter 1

1. William Coxe, *Memoirs of the Life and Administration of Sir Robert Walpole, Earl of Orford*, Volumes 3–4 (London: Longman, Hurst, Rees, Orme, & Brown, 1816), p. 115.
2. *Cobbett's Political Register*, 27 November 1830.
3. E.P. Thompson, *The Making of the English Working Class* (London: Vintage, 1966), p. 68.

Chapter 2

1. Paul Gregg, Susan Harkness and Stephen Machin, 'Poor Kids: Trends in Child Poverty in Britain, 1968–96', *Fiscal Studies*, vol. 20, no. 2 (1999), pp. 163–87.
2. Cited in Daniel Dorling, Jan Rigby et al., *Poverty, Wealth and Place in Britain, 1968 to 2005* (Bristol: Joseph Rowntree Foundation, 2007), p. 2.
3. 'The Impact of the Poll Tax in Manchester' (pamphlet), Citizens Advice Bureau Experience, February–July 1990.
4. John Campbell, *Margaret Thatcher, Volume 2: The Iron Lady* (London: Vintage, 2008), p. 372–3.
5. Conservative Party Election Manifesto, October 1974.
6. David Butler, Andrew Adonis and Tony Travers, *Failure in British Government: The Politics of the Poll Tax* (Oxford: Oxford University Press, 1994), p. 32.
7. *Financial Times*, 17 April 1982.
8. Odd-Helge Fjeldstad and Ole Therkildsen, 'Mass Taxation and State-Society Relations in East Africa', in Deborah Brautigam, Odd-Helge Fjeldstad and Mick Moore, *Taxation and State-Building in Developing Countries* (Cambridge: Cambridge University Press, 2008), p. 115.

9. Fjeldstad and Therkildsen, 'Mass Taxation', p. 116.
10. Christopher D. Foster, *British Government in Crisis, or, The Third English Revolution* (London: Hart Publishing, 2005), pp. 102–3.
11. Kenneth Baker, *The Turbulent Years* (London: Faber & Faber, 1993), p. 122.
12. Foster, *British Government in Crisis*, p. 104.
13. Conservative Party Election Manifesto, October 1974 (emphasis mine).
14. Cited in Stewart Lansley, Sue Goss, Christian Wolfram, *Councils in Conflict: The Rise and Fall of the Municipal Left* (Basingstoke: Macmillan, 1989), p. 186.
15. Margaret Thatcher, *The Downing Street Years* (London: HarperCollins, 1993), p. 654.
16. Adam Smith, *An Inquiry Into the Nature and Causes of the Wealth of Nations*, Volume 2, (New Delhi: Atlantic, 2008), p. 777.
17. Cited in Geoffrey Fry, *The Politics of the Thatcher Revolution: An Interpretation of British Politics 1979–1990* (London: Springer, 2008), p. 175.
18. Campbell, *Margaret Thatcher, Volume 2*, p. 483.
19. Michael Heseltine, *Life in the Jungle* (London: Hodder and Stoughton, 2000), p. 353.
20. 'The "Semi-Detached" Member of Margaret Thatcher's Cabinet', *The Spectator*, 18 January 2014.
21. Foster, *British Government in Crisis*, p. 104 fn.
22. Alan Clarke, *Diaries: In Power 1983–1992* (London: Phoenix, 1994), p. 287.
23. Michael Portillo, House of Commons written answers, 27 January 1988, Col 270.
24. 'Tories Clash on Poll Tax', *Independent*, 7 July 1987.
25. Louise Phillips, 'Hegemony of the Political Discourse: The Lasting Impact of Thatcherism', *Sociology Journal*, vol. 32, no. 4 (1998), pp. 854–6.
26. *Local Council Review: Journal of the National Association of Local Councils* (Winter 1989), pp. 78–9.
27. Simon Jenkins, *Thatcher and Sons: A Revolution in Three Acts* (London: Penguin, 2007), p. 174.
28. Hansard, 15 February 1989.
29. Michael Lavalette and Gerry Mooney, *Class Struggle and Social Welfare* (Abingdon: Routledge, 2000), pp. 210–11.
30. *Financial Times*, 16 March 1990.
31. William Waldegrave, *A Different Kind Of Weather: A Memoir* (London: Constable, 2015), p. 237.
32. Local Government Information UNIT (LGIU) *Poll Tax News*, Issue 6 (May 1988).
33. CIPFA, 'Women and the Poll Tax', 1987, p. 4.
34. LGIU, 'Guide to the Poll Tax', p. 43.
35. ALA, 'Black People, Ethnic Minorities and the Poll Tax', p. 5.
36. On 5 May 1987: 'One will pay a good deal less poll tax if one lives in a good Tory authority area than if one lives in a Labour authority area.'
37. Department for the Environment leaflet from April 1989.
38. Heseltine, *Life in the Jungle*, p. 353.

39. 'Tory MPs Cheer Rates Reform Plan', *The Times*, 29 January 1986.
40. 'Parliament and Politics: Cross-party Unease Over Poll Tax', *Financial Times*, 9 May 1985.
41. David Torrance, *'We in Scotland': Thatcherism in a Cold Climate* (Edinburgh: Birlinn, 2009), p. 143.
42. *Sunday Times*, 1 April 1990, cited in Torrance, *'We in Scotland'*, p. 144.
43. Alan Watkins, *A Conservative Coup: The Fall of Margaret Thatcher* (London: Gerald Duckworth, 1992), p. 67.
44. Tony Travers, 'Local Government: Margaret Thatcher's 11-year War', *Guardian*, 9 April 2013.
45. Ben Jackson and Robert Saunders (eds), *Making Thatcher's Britain* (Cambridge: Cambridge University Press, 2012), p. 140.
46. Conservative Party Election Manifesto 1987.
47. Edgar Wilson, *A Very British Miracle: The Failure of Thatcherism* (London: Pluto, 1992), p. 109.
48. Cited in 'This Far and No Further' (pamphlet), Strathclyde Anti Poll Tax Federation, 1989.
49. Campbell, *Margaret Thatcher, Volume 2*, p. 559.
50. Cited in John Gibson, *The Politics and Economics of the Poll Tax: Mrs Thatcher's Downfall* (London: Emas, 1990), p. 218.
51. Danny Burns, *Poll Tax Rebellion* (Stirling: AK Press/Attack International, 1992).
52. Gibson, *The Politics and Economics of the Poll Tax*, pp. 206–7.
53. Gibson, *The Politics and Economics of the Poll Tax*, p. 203.
54. P. Richards, 'The Recent History of Local Fiscal Reform', in S. Bailey and R. Addison (eds), *The Reform of Local Government Finance in Britain* (Abingdon: Routledge, 1988), p. 25.

Chapter 3

1. *Daily Record*, 13 January 1987.
2. Thatcher, *The Downing Street Years*, p. 651.
3. Torrance, *'We in Scotland'*, p. 147.
4. 'Downing Street Files Reveal How Oliver Letwin Kept Poll Tax Plans Alive', *Guardian*, 30 December 2014.
5. Keith Laybourn, *Marxism in Britain: Dissent, Decline and Re-emergence 1945–c.2000* (Abingdon: Routledge, 2006), pp. 137–8.
6. Richard Bellamy, 'The Anti-Poll Tax Non-Payment Campaign and Liberal Concepts of Political Obligation', *Government and Opposition*, vol. 29, no. 1 (1994), p. 31.
7. John Maxton, 'Poll Tax: A Solution Far Worse Than the Problem', *Glasgow Herald*, 13 February 1987.
8. Tommy Sheridan and Joan McAlpine, *A Time to Rage* (Edinburgh: Polygon, 1994), p. 70.
9. Burns, *Poll Tax Rebellion*, p. 25.
10. *Marxism Today*, May 1990, p. 27.

11. Burns, *Poll Tax Rebellion*, p. 33.
12. *Class War*, Issue 29, 1988 p. 6.
13. *Lancashire Evening Post*, 8 October 1988.
14. *Scotland on Sunday*, 18 September 1988.
15. Report of the 87th Annual Conference of the Labour Party, p. 46.
16. *Socialist Worker*, 20 August 1988.
17. *Socialist Worker*, 26 October 1988.
18. According to surveys published in *The Scotsman*, 11 March 1988 and 20 September 1988.
19. 'The Night SNP Turned Red Clydeside Yellow in Govan and Set Scotland on New Political Path', *Daily Record*, 4 November 2018.
20. Statement in the House of Commons, 21 July 1987.
21. 'Beating the Poll Tax' (pamphlet), Anarchist Federation, 1990.
22. Official Report of the Standing Committees: Session, Volume 6, p. 129.
23. Cited in Andy McSmith, *No Such Thing as Society* (London: Constable and Robinson, 2010), p. 278.
24. Andrew Neil, *Full Disclosure* (Basingstoke: Macmillan, 1996), p. 243.

Chapter 4

1. Thomas Docherty, *Alterities: Criticism, History, Representation* (Oxford: Clarendon Press, 1996), p. 185.
2. 'How to Beat the Poll Tax', *Socialist Organiser*, 1989, p. 4.
3. 'Poll Tax is History', *Guardian*, 14 April 1999.
4. LGIU, *Poll Tax News*, Issue 6 (May 1988).
5. LGIU, *Poll Tax News*, Issue 9 (September 1988).
6. ABAPTF Bulletin, no. 4 (June 1990).
7. Keith Aitken, *The Bairns o' Adam: The Story of the STUC* (Edinburgh: Polygon, 1997), p. 298.
8. LGIU, *Poll Tax News*, Issue 7 (June 1988).
9. Quoted in *Independent*, 15 September 1988.
10. GLATUC, 'Guide to the Trade Union Policies on the Poll Tax', 1988.
11. Mike Ironside and Roger Seifert, *Facing Up to Thatcherism: The History of NALGO, 1979–1993* (Oxford: Oxford University Press, 2000), p. 299.
12. Ironside and Seifert, *Facing Up to Thatcherism*, p. 253.
13. Ironside and Seifert, *Facing Up to Thatcherism*, p. 299.
14. *The Militant*, 16 June 1989.
15. Cited by Richard Murgatroyd in 'The Popular Politics of the Poll Tax: An Active Citizenship of the Left?', unpublished PhD thesis.
16. AWG (leaflet), 'The Poll Tax: A Strategy to Win'.
17. Anarchist Communist Federation, 'Beating the Poll Tax' (1990), p. 7.
18. 'How to Beat the Poll Tax', *Socialist Organiser*, p. 3.
19. Workers' Power, 'The Great Poll Tax Robbery' (1990), p. 5.
20. *Financial Times*, 1 April 1989.
21. Citizens Advice Bureau Experience, 'The Impact of the Poll Tax in Manchester' (February–July 1990), p. 35.

22. For more on this see Ewan Gibbs, 'Historical Tradition and Community Mobilisation: Narratives of Red Clydeside in Memories of the Anti Poll Tax Movement in Scotland, 1988–1990', *Labor History*, vol. 57 (2016).
23. *Nottingham Evening Post*, 8 March 1989.

Chapter 5

1. 'The Poll Tax 20 Years On', *The Scotsman*, 26 March 2009.
2. *Financial Times*, 2 February 1989.
3. 'Poll Tax: Who is Going to Pay?', *Socialist Outlook*, 1990.
4. National Federation of Anti-Poll Tax Groups, *Stop the Poll Tax*, Issue 4.
5. Paul Hoggett and Danny Burns, 'The Revenge of the Poor: The Anti-Poll Tax Campaign in Britain', *Critical Social Policy*, vol. 11, no. 33 (1991), p. 96.
6. 'Stannary' refers to tin-mining districts in Devon and Cornwall.
7. 'Cornish Poll Tax Rebel Barred', *The Times*, 23 March 1990.
8. Quoted in Sally Brown, *Diary of a People's Marcher: An Account of the People's March Against the Poll Tax* (Liverpool: Anteus Graphics, 1991), p. 10.
9. 'The Poll Tax 20 Years On' *The Scotsman*, 26 March 2009.
10. *Scotland on Sunday*, December 3, 1989.
11. 'The Poll Tax 20 Years On', *The Scotsman*, 26 March 2009.
12. 'The Poll Tax 20 Years On', *The Scotsman*, 26 March 2009.
13. *Glasgow Herald*, 12 February 1991.
14. 'The Poll Tax 20 Years On', *The Scotsman*, 26 March 2009.
15. See http://www.anthonycgreen.com/109520654.
16. Tony Benn, *The End of an Era: Diaries 1980–90* (London: Hutchinson 1990), p. 560.
17. *Coventry Evening Telegraph*, 29 June 1989.
18. Maureen Reynolds, *Uncollectable: The Story of the Poll Tax Revolt* (Salford: Manchester Anti-Poll Tax Federation, 1992), pp. 26–8.
19. *Dispatch*, 8 December 1989.
20. *Dispatch*, 15 December 1989.
21. 'Poll Tax Versus People Power!', *Eastbourne and District Advertiser*, 1 February 1990.
22. Andy Winter, Jean Calder, Sheila Hall, Kate Packham, Richard Stanton, Mark Thompson and Hordon Wingate all refused to pay.
23. 'Poll Tax to Go Up in Smoke', *Evening Argus*, 5 April 1990.
24. Unpublished manuscript by Maureen Reynolds, Modern Resource Centre, 601/E/6/6.
25. *Surrey Herald*, 15 March 1990.
26. *Evening Argus*, 2 March 1990.
27. *Evening Chronicle*, 14 March 1990.
28. '250 March to Join Park Poll Tax Demo', *Worthing Herald*, 23 March 1990.
29. Paul Bagguley, 'Protest, Poverty and Power: a case study of the anti-poll tax movement', *The Sociological Review*, vol. 43, no. 4 (1995), p. 699.
30. *The Times*, 6 March 1990.
31. Leaflet from the Colchester 17 Defence Campaign.

32. 'A Peoples' Account of the Hackney Anti-Poll Tax Demonstration on March 8th 1990' (pamphlet), Hackney Community Defence Association, 1990.
33. Bagguley, 'Protest, Poverty and Power', p. 698.
34. Sheridan and McAlpine, *A Time to Rage*, p. 116.
35. *Guardian*, 10 March 1990.
36. Leaflet from the Direct Action Movement.
37. *Nottingham Evening Post*, 9 March 1990.
38. 'Thatcher Hits at Militant Over Poll Tax', *The Times*, 9 March 1990.
39. 'Thatcher Hits at Militant Over Poll Tax', *The Times*, 9 March 1990.
40. *Glasgow Herald*, 2 March 1990.
41. Reynolds, *Uncollectable*, p. 55.
42. Michael Lavalette and George Mooney, 'Undermining the "North-South Divide"? Fighting the Poll Tax in Scotland, England and Wales', *Critical Social Policy*, vol. 10, no. 29 (1990), pp. 110–11.
43. Gibson, *The Politics and Economics of the Poll Tax*, Chapter 5.
44. Citizens Advice Bureau Experience, 'The Impact of the Poll Tax in Manchester' (February–July 1990), p. 8.
45. *Independent*, 21 May 1990.
46. 'MPs Defy Poll Tax Warrants', *The Herald*, 18 January 1990.
47. *The Times*, 11 March 1989.
48. Peter Taaffe, *Rise of 'Militant': Thirty Years of 'Militant'* (London: Militant Publications, 1995), p. 374–5.
49. *Tribune*, 9 March 1990.
50. *Tribune*, 5 February 1988.
51. *Tribune*, 7 April 1989.
52. *Scotland on Sunday*, 2 July 1989.
53. Isle of Wight Labour Party, press release, 5 December 1989.

Chapter 6

1. *Marxism Today*, May 1990, p. 27.
2. Tony Benn, *The End of An Era: Diaries 1980–1990* (London: Random House, 2012), pp. 585–6.
3. Sheridan and McAlpine, *A Time to Rage*, p. 126.
4. 'Poll Tax Riot: 10 Hours That Shook Trafalgar Square' (pamphlet), ACAB Press, 1990, p. 33.
5. See www.revoltagainstplenty.com/index.php/archive-local/42-the-london-poll-tax-riot-of-1990.html.
6. 'Militant Link to Poll Tax Demo – London Riot', *The Sunday Times*, 1 April 1990.
7. Police reports from the various demonstrations obtained under a Freedom of Information request by Solomon Hughes, available online at http://specialbranchfiles.uk/poll-tax-story.
8. See https://crab.wordpress.com/2010/03/30/the-battle-of-trafalgar-the-poll-tax-riot-20-years-on.
9. Tony Benn, *The Benn Diaries* (London: Random House, 2017), p. 924.

10. Comment made on Facebook history group, The Anti-Poll Tax Campaign 1987–1991.
11. Sheridan and McAlpine, *A Time to Rage*, p. 127.
12. 'Poll Tax Riot: 10 Hours That Shook Trafalgar Square', ACAB Press, p. 20.
13. Editorial, *Living Marxism*, May 1990.
14. Sheridan and McAlpine, *A Time to Rage*, p. 132.
15. Sheridan and McAlpine, *A Time to Rage*, p. 126.
16. *Financial Times*, 2 April 1990; *Glasgow Herald*, 2 April 1990.
17. 'The Poll Tax 20 Years On', *The Scotsman*, 26 March 2009.
18. See http://campaignopposingpolicesurveillance.com/2018/03/31/1990-spycop-john-dines-boasts-of-his-poll-tax-arrest.
19. Clarke, *Diaries: In Power 1983–1992*, p. 290.
20. Hansard, 2 April 1990.
21. Eileen Jones, *Neil Kinnock* (London: Robert Hale, 1994), p. 143.
22. 'Fury at Statement on Poll Tax Rioting', *Scottish Herald*, 3 April 1990.
23. Tony Benn, *The Benn Diaries 1940–1990* (London: Arrow, 1995), p. 625.

Chapter 7

1. Hoggett and Burns, 'The Revenge of the Poor', p. 96.
2. 'Tax Rebels State Demo at Court Hearings', *Leader*, 23 August 1990.
3. 'Poll Tax "Hero" Does a Runner', *Newham Recorder*, 21 November 1991.
4. 'Storm Over Poll Tax Prosecutions', *East Kent Mercury*, 30 August 1990.
5. *The Magistrate*, July–August 1990.
6. LGIU, *Poll Tax Focus*, March 1990.
7. Eastbourne Anti-Poll Tax Newsletter, June 1991.
8. Interview with Steve Nally.
9. *West Sussex Gazette*, 2 May 1990.
10. Richard Heffernan and Mike Marqusee, *Defeat from the Jaws of Victory* (London: Pluto, 1992), p. 294.
11. Sheridan and McAlpine, *A Time to Rage*, p. 211.
12. Heffernan and Marqusee, *Defeat from the Jaws of Victory*, p. 295.
13. Heffernan and Marqusee *Defeat from the Jaws of Victory*, p . 295.
14. See www.westoverward.co.uk/on-this-day-in-history-july-12th-1990-the-victoria-anti-poll-tax-by-election.
15. LGIU, *Poll Tax Focus Extra* (April 1990), p. 5.
16. Hansard, 11 July 1990.
17. *The Times*, 20 July 1990.
18. 'Poll Tax Axe Draws Blood', *Guardian*, 2 August 1990.
19. *The Times*, 9 July 1990.
20. *Nottingham Evening Post*, 6 March 1990.
21. Local leaflet Nottingham APTU.
22. *Independent on Sunday*, 3 June 1990.
23. Institute of Public Finance, *Progress on the Collection of the Community Charge* (London: Institute of Public Finance, 1991).
24. *Guardian*, 1 March 1991.

25. *Evening Argus*, 11 July 1990.
26. Burns, *Poll Tax Rebellion*, pp. 65–6.
27. *Evening Argus*, 14 April 1990.
28. *Daily Express*, 10 September 1987.
29. *Arun Gazette*, 3 August 1990.
30. 'The Poll Tax 20 Years On', *The Scotsman*, 26 March 2009.
31. Hoggett and Burns, 'The Revenge of the Poor', p. 99.
32. Sheridan and McAlpine, *A Time to Rage*, p. 168.
33. 3D Newsletter, October 1990.
34. Brown, *Dairy of a People's Marcher*, p. 43.
35. Brown, *Dairy of a People's Marcher*, p. 46.
36. Brown, *Dairy of a People's Marcher*, pp. 108–9.
37. *We Beat the Poll Tax*, Militant Publications, http://www.socialistparty.org.uk/polltax/p2frame.htm?ch43.htm.
38. In a tragic ironic comment on the times, the ship was called 'The Spirit of Free Enterprise', and many of the dead had taken advantage of a cheap holiday offer from the Conservative-supporting *Sun* newspaper.
39. *The Times*, 5 May 1990.
40. Clarke, *Diaries: In Power 1983–1992*, p. 345.
41. Market and Opinion Research International, 26 November 1990.
42. Michael Crick and Adrian Van Klaveren, 'Mrs Thatcher's Greatest Blunder', *Contemporary Record*, vol. 5, no. 3 (1991), p. 398.
43. Waldegrave, *A Different Kind of Weather: A Memoir*, p. 238.

Chapter 8

1. Documents archived at Sparrow's Nest, www.thesparrowsnest.org.uk/collections/public_archive/6131.pdf.
2. Papers from the second ABAPTF conference, 1990.
3. Lavalette and Mooney, 'Undermining the "North-South Divide"?', p. 112.
4. Sheridan and McAlpine, *A Time to Rage*, p. 163.
5. Sheridan and McAlpine, *A Time to Rage*, p. 162.
6. Jones, *Neil Kinnock*, p. 158.
7. Reynolds, *Uncollectable*, p. 100.
8. 'Poll Tax Pooch', *Daily Star*, 27 April 1991.
9. 'Tories Prepare to Scrap Flagship', *Financial Times*, 21 February 1991.
10. *Guardian*, 21 February 1991.
11. Wilson, *A Very British Miracle*, p. 111.
12. *Financial Times*, 16 March 1991.
13. Sheridan and McAlpine, *A Time to Rage*, p. 265.
14. Taaffe, The *Rise of Militant*, p. 238.
15. 'How the Militant Was Built – and How It Was Destroyed', *Socialist Appeal*, 10 October 2004.
16. Sheridan and McAlpine, *A Time to Rage*, p. 196.
17. Sheridan and McAlpine, *A Time to Rage*, p. 202.
18. Personal correspondence with the author.

19. Poll Tax Law Review – Computer Evidence Special, 1992, p. 1.
20. 'Labour Pounces', *Morning Star*, 23 March 1991.
21. *Evening Argus*, 25 September 1990.
22. Quotes taken from the Streatham CLP newsletter 'The Windmill'.
23. *London Fight the Poll Tax*, Issue 14 (March 1992).
24. *Independent on Sunday*, 22 and 29 January 1995.
25. Quoted in *Independent*, 23 January 1995.
26. *Independent*, 21 August 1994.
27. 'The Quality of Justice: The Imprisonment of Those Who Failed to Pay Their Poll Tax Raises Fundamental Questions About Standards of Justice', *The Law Gazette*, 8 February 1995.
28. 'Alex Salmond to Ban Scottish Councils from Chasing Historic Poll Tax Debts', *Guardian*, 2 October 2014.

Chapter 9

1. Butler, Adonis and Travers, *Failure in British Government*, p. 298.
2. 'Reflections on Britain's Student Movement', 2 March 2012, at www.opendemocracy.net/en/opendemocracyuk/reflections-on-britains-student-movement.
3. 'The Great Anti-Poll Tax Victory', 26 February 2010, at https://www.socialistparty.org.uk/articles/8910/26-02-2010/anti-poll-tax-victory-how-18-million-people-brought-down-thatcher.
4. Heseltine, *Life in the Jungle*, p. 389.
5. Timothy Besley, Ian Preston and Michael Ridge, 'Fiscal Anarchy in the UK: Modelling Poll Tax Noncompliance', *Journal of Public Economics*, vol. 64, no. 2 (1997), pp. 137–52.
6. See Simon Hannah, *A Party With Socialists In It: A History of the Labour Left* (London: Pluto, 2018).
7. Colin Barker, 'Class Struggle and Social Movements', in Colin Barker et al. (eds), *Marxism and Social Movements* (Chicago: Haymarket, 2014), p. 52.
8. 'Is It Right to Break the Law?', *New York Times*, 12 January 1964.
9. Remarks opening Glasgow Shopping Centre (Militant inspired riot in Hackney), at www.margaretthatcher.org/document/108033.
10. Jürgen Habermas, *Legitimation Crisis* (Boston: Beacon Press, 1975).
11. See, for instance, his essay on Thatcherism in *Marxism Today*, February 1980.
12. Karl Marx, 'The Trial of the Rhenish District Committee of Democrats', *Neue Rheinische Zeitung*, nos. 231 and 232 (1849).
13. Gibbs, 'Historical Tradition and Community Mobilisation', p. 2.
14. 'Poll Tax: Who is Going to Pay?', *Socialist Outlook*, 1990.
15. Paul Byrne, *Social Movements in Britain* (Abingdon: Routledge, 1997), p. 23.
16. David McCrone, '"Excessive and Unreasonable": The Politics of the Poll Tax in Scotland', *International Journal of Urban and Regional Research*, vol. 15, no. 3 (1991), p. 452.
17. Personal correspondence with the author.

18. See, for instance, Claus Offe, 'New Social Movements: Challenging the Boundaries of Institutional Politics', *Social Research*, vol. 52, no. 4 (1985), pp. 817–68.
19. Bagguley, 'Protest, Poverty and Power', p. 697.
20. André Gorz, *Farewell to the Working Class* (London: Pluto Press, 1982), pp. 80–1.
21. Martin Jacques, 'Thatcherism – The Impasse Broken?', *Marxism Today*, October 1979, p. 13.
22. Joshua Clover, *Riot. Strike. Riot: The New Era of Uprisings* (London: Verso, 2019), pp. 8–17.
23. Bagguley, 'Protest, Poverty and Power', p. 697.
24. John Krinsky, 'Marxism and the Politics of Possibility', in Barker et al., *Marxism and Social Movements*, p. 107.
25. Krinsky, 'Marxism and the Politics of Possibility', p. 108.
26. E.P. Thompson, 'Eighteenth-century English Society: Class Struggle Without Class?', *Social History*, vol. 3, no. 2 (1978), p. 149.
27. E.P. Thompson, 'The Peculiarities of the English', *Socialist Register*, 1965, p. 357.
28. Gibbs, 'Historical Tradition and Community Mobilisation'.
29. Sheridan and McAlpine, *A Time to Rage*, p. 177.
30. See https://www.marxists.org/archive/marx/works/1845/german-ideology/cho1b.htm.

Conclusion

1. Arthur Midwinter, 'Economic Theory, the Poll Tax and Local Spending', *Politics*, vol. 9 (1989), pp. 9–15.
2. Gibson, *The Politics and Economics of the Poll Tax*, p. 248.
3. See Hannah, *A Party With Socialists In It*.
4. Keith Laybourn and Christine F. Collette, *Modern Britain Since 1979: A Reader* (London: I.B. Taurus, 2003), p. 154.
5. Peter Kenway, 'Labour and Tory Councils are Choosing the Poll Tax Over the Safety Net', *New Statesman*, 8 April 2014.
6. 'The Great British Council Tax Scandal – a Big Issue Investigation', *The Big Issue*, April 2017.
7. 'Living in Fear of the Bailiffs' Knock on the Door', *Financial Times*, 21 June 2019.

Index

The Pluto Press Newsletter

Hello friend of Pluto!

Want to stay on top of the best radical books
we publish?

Then sign up to be the first to hear about our
new books, as well as special events,
podcasts and videos.

You'll also get 50% off your first order with us
when you sign up.

Come and join us!

Go to bit.ly/PlutoNewsletter